Journey Together Towards First Holy Communion

Resources for catechists accompanying parents of
children preparing to celebrate First Holy Communion

PADDY RYLANDS

Kevin
Mayhew

First published in 2000 in Great Britain by
KEVIN MAYHEW LTD
Buxhall
Stowmarket, Suffolk IP14 3BW

ISBN 1 84003 608 7
Catalogue No 1500380

0 1 2 3 4 5 6 7 8 9

Cover design by Jonathan Stroulger
Edited by Helen Elliot
Typesetting by Louise Selfe
Printed in Great Britain

About the Author

For twenty years Paddy Rylands has worked with catechists involved in sacramental preparation, first of all in the parish of Our Lady and St Joseph, Hanwell, and for the past fourteen years as a member of Shrewsbury Diocese Education Service where she is adviser for parish and adult formation.

Foreword

It is good to be able to welcome and recommend this publication. Its aim is to offer practical help in addressing the important role of parents and parish in the preparation of our children for the Sacraments, and its starting point is the recognition that all of us need to grow in appreciation of these Sacraments. They are gifts of God to his people, inviting us and enabling us to enter more fully into the Paschal Mystery of Jesus. Responding is a life-long affair. One of the many strengths of this book is that it sees the time of First Celebration of the Sacrament as an opportunity for all concerned to deepen that response. Material to enable catechists and parents to do so forms the main content of these pages.

What we are given, however, is not so much a programme to be worked through as a process with which to operate. Given that all of us are at different stages in understanding and responding to the Sacraments, the emphasis here is on discovering what material is appropriate for both catechists and parents. A variety of resources are made available but the need for adaptation to meet specific needs is constantly urged. There is no alternative but to meet people where they are and to start from there. What is important is that appropriate help is available to take the next possible step forward in understanding and response.

It is impossible to read this book and not realise that it comes from the pen of a 'hands on' practitioner. Heeding its advice and its eye for detail in planning will ensure that many a pitfall is avoided. I recommend it and hope it will be used widely.

Brian M. Noble
Bishop of Shrewsbury
June, 2000

For Norah
and all Companions on the Journey in Hanwell,
in Shrewsbury Diocese and in Peru.

With grateful thanks and appreciation:

to the many people whose support and practical help have made this book possible;

to Bishop Brian Noble, Peter Morgan, Rosemary McCloskey and June Edwards who prepared resources for this book;

and with immeasurable thanks to Rowena Nield for her painstaking typing, preparation and proof-reading of the manuscript.

Contents _____

PART 1. Guidelines for Catechists

PART 2. Resources for Eucharist

PART 1
Guidelines for Catechists

Remember that we are listened to with much greater satisfaction when we ourselves are enjoying our work; for what we say is affected by the very joy of which we ourselves are aware, and it proceeds from us with greater ease and with more acceptance . . . The important thing is that everyone should enjoy catechising; for the better we succeed in this the more attractive we shall be.

The rule which is to be our guide is not difficult to find. For if in material matters God loves a cheerful giver (1 Corinthians 9:7), how much more will he in spiritual matters? But the certainty that this joy will be with us at the right time is something that depends on the mercy of the one who has given us this teaching.

St Augustine on 'Catechising the Uninstructed' in Jean Comby, *How to Read Church History*, volume 1.

Using these Resources

1. Working with Parents

These resources are planned for use with parents of children preparing to celebrate the Sacrament of First Holy Communion. It is anticipated that they

- form but one part of the parish's overall provision of adult catechesis and are organised in the light of this;
- take into account what the parish offers to parents both *before* and *after* preparation for the Sacrament;
- reflect an awareness of the way school and parish work in partnership.

They are intended for *adaptation*.

To be used most appropriately, it is presumed that the catechist

- knows her/his parents, their questions and concerns, their experience of adult catechesis, of group work
- is 'at home' with the theme and familiar with the relevant scripture passages, Church traditions and teachings
- is familiar with the catechetical process on which the material is based, that is
  a. inviting participants to name and then reflect on their personal experience of the particular theme
  b. offering appropriate 'input', sharing the Church's teachings/traditions
  c. allowing time for further reflection leading towards an integration of what has been shared into the lives of participants
  d. celebrating.

(This way of working is described as the 'Pastoral Cycle'. A more detailed explanation is given on page 29.)

For each session material is offered from which the catechist can make a selection so that the needs and situations of the particular group of parents are truly met. If the catechist is to accompany others on their faith journey, the starting point is the reality of *their* lives – the journey begins with the parents.

There is a variety of ways of working with parents as they prepare to celebrate sacraments:

- on an individual basis
- in small group clusters
- as a large group, meeting in either the school or parish hall.

These resources are prepared for the larger group meeting, but can be easily adapted to use either with smaller groups or as points for discussion with individual families.

They are intended for *adaptation*.

2. Accompanying Parents as their children prepare to celebrate sacraments

These resources for have been prepared on the understanding that
- parents, in general, want the best and will do their best for their children
- school, parish and family can be powerful influences on children growing in faith, particularly when they work in partnership
- a child's time of preparation for sacraments is a 'ripe' occasion to offer to parents an invitation to participate in a programme of adult catechesis
- adults have *the right* to catechesis (*Catechesi Tradendae,* para. 64, Catholic Truth Society, 1979)
- many adults appreciate the opportunity: to reflect on their faith with others, to share their questions and concerns, to update themselves with the tradition and teachings of the Church
- parents enjoy, as well as find helpful, the opportunity to discuss with other parents ways of sharing faith with their children.

The role of parents as catechists of their children is considered to be of great importance in the Church:

> It goes without saying that Christian parents are the primary and irreplaceable catechists of their children.
>
> *Christifideles Laici,* para. 34
> Catholic Truth Society, 1988

In Pope John Paul II's address to the parents of First Communicants at Cardiff, he emphasises their vital part in bringing up their children 'in the ways of faith':

> Dear parents of these children: your love for Christ has made this day possible. For you are your children's first teachers in the ways of faith. By what you say and do, you show them the truths of our faith and the values of the Gospel. This is indeed not only a sacred duty, but a grace, a great privilege. Many other members of the Church share in this task, but the main responsibility for your children's religious formation rests upon your shoulders. So try to make your homes genuinely Christian. Help your children to grow and mature as Jesus did at Nazareth, 'in wisdom, in stature and in favour with God and men' (Luke 2:52). Allow no one to take advantage of their lack of experience and knowledge. As you share with them in their personal pilgrimage to God, may you always be united in prayer and worship and in humble love of God and his people.
>
> *The Pope Teaches – The Pope in Britain*
> Catholic Truth Society, 1982

But it is not just children who benefit:

> The parents themselves profit from the effort that this demands of them, for in a catechetical dialogue of this sort, each individual both receives and gives.
>
> *Catechesi Tradendae*, para. 68
> Catholic Truth Society, 1979

The question, 'Who supports and catechises the parents?' needs to be addressed. If it is accepted

- that catechesis is the 'right of all believers' *(Catechesi Tradendae*, para. 64)
- that the parish is the 'pre-eminent place for catechesis' *(Catechesi Tradendae*, para. 67)
- that adult catechesis is the 'principal form' *(Catechesi Tradendae*, para. 43)

then those involved in leadership in the parish are called to give serious consideration and reflection to the catechesis being offered to adults, especially to parents with children preparing to celebrate sacraments.

You might find it helpful to read:

'Congregation for the Clergy', *General Directory for Catechesis*, Catholic Truth Society, 1997.

---

3. Offering Catechesis to Adults in the Parish – some possibilities

Based on a vision of inviting parishioners to participate in catechesis, the 'right of all believers', on a number of occasions during their lifelong journey in faith, either individually, in small groups, in family clusters or in larger groups within the community setting; inviting participants to a deeper relationship with Christ.

When preparing to celebrate sacraments
For adults as parents, sponsors, godparents or members of the parish team:
  Infant Baptism
  Confirmation
  First Communion
  Reconciliation

For adults, as candidates, sponsors, godparents or members of the parish team:
  The Rite of Christian Initiation of Adults
  Marriage

Additional opportunities for parents
  Mothers' and toddlers' groups
  'Coffee and chat' groups the year children start school
  Parenting programmes – the year either preceding or following the celebration of First Sacraments
  Another look at First Sacraments – when children are in Year 5
  Moving on – from primary to secondary school
  Teen-parenting programme – for parents of teenagers

Ministry training
In particular,
  Special ministers of the Eucharist
  Bereavement visitors
  Readers
  Liturgy teams
  Catechists
  Parish pastoral councils

'Life crisis' moments
In particular,
  Bereavement
  Divorce, marriage break-up
  Redundancy, unemployment, early retirement

Ongoing adult groups
(Based on the liturgical year)
  Bible study
  Senior citizens' faithsharing/prayer groups

'Reflections on the faith', e.g. short 5 or 6 week course or monthly sessions on
   aspects of Church teachings
Parishioners with disabilities
Family life
Local community issues

If the sessions are to be *catechetical*, the kinds of material and resources used will vary according to the participants
- their stage along their faith journey
- their questions, hopes and expectations
- their level of literacy
- their previous catechetical experience
- the time they can give.

You might find it helpful to read:
Adult Catechesis in the Christian Community, International Council for Catechesis, St Pauls Publishing, 1990.

4. Parents' Sessions in Context

In preparing to celebrate sacraments, there are some recognisable elements in a parish programme:

Candidates' preparation
- with their family
- with their teacher
- with their catechist
- with their parish community

Parents' preparation
- providing information about the candidates' preparation with an invitation and suggestions of how to support this at home
- looking at aspects of parenting, e.g. how to pray with children
- adult catechesis – accompanying adults on *their* faith journey

Liturgy
- celebrating stages along the journey of preparation.

Parish community involvement
- providing welcome, nurture, support, witness, prayer for the candidates and their families.

Pastoral visiting
- meeting families in their homes – reaching out, befriending, inviting, supporting, healing.

Team meetings
- offering initial and ongoing formation, leading to working in unison, better communication as well as personal growth and faith development.

In planning Parents' Sessions it is essential to consider the following:
- how the proposed meetings fit into/relate to the total preparation: candidates' preparation, liturgical celebrations, parish community involvement, family visiting, team meetings
- the involvement of families not attending the parish school
- the involvement of families with children with learning disabilities
- the parents' sessions themselves: the place and timing of meetings, the content of meetings, the choice of themes, the team involved.

Family Links (see page 15) can be a useful source of contact with families.

You might find it helpful to read *Sharing the Gift,* Paddy Rylands, Collins Liturgical Publications, 1989.

---

5. Family Links

Purpose

- to be a personal and direct link between the family and the parish community
- to be a support
- to be able to follow through any queries, problems as they emerge on a personal family level
- to help with communication
- to liaise with the parish priest and programme co-ordinator as appropriate.

NB: The link person is not intended to be a pastoral counsellor, solver of problems or go-between, but rather to enable the family to have an appropriate relationship with the parish so that the best preparation for first sacraments can take place.

Organisation

- each Family Link to link with a cluster of 4 to 5 families, preferably living in their neighbourhood.

Contact with families

- to deliver an invitation to enrol for the programme, and be able to explain the proposed preparation, responding to any queries
- to deliver an invitation to the first Parents' Session
- to welcome parents to the first session
- to introduce them to others in the 'cluster' group
- to take responsibility for gathering specific information, e.g. details of baptism, names for the certificate, etc., as requested by the programme co-ordinator
- to inform and invite families to participate in specific 'family' events in the parish
- to maintain contact, visiting as appropriate during the course of the year.

Who are the links?

- willing parishioners
- parents who have experienced the programme
- catechists
- parish sisters
- priests
- volunteers who have time, an ability to listen, are warm, friendly, non-judgemental, able to keep confidences, and have the good of these families at heart.

Formation for Family Links

- a clarification of the purpose, role and task
- basic listening skills
- an introduction to visiting skills
- an understanding of the overall preparation for First Sacraments

Planning and Preparation _____

1. Initial Planning

A framework for schools and parishes to use when planning their programme

How are families invited to participate?

- letter from the parish priest?
- letter from the parish catechist?
- letter from school?
- visit from the parish priest?
- visit from the parish catechist?
- contact with the class teacher?
- parish newsletter?

What commitment is expected from parents?

- supporting their child's catechesis?
- bringing their child to Mass?
- full participation in the programme?

How is this to be formalised?

- Enrolment Mass?
- enrolment form?
- interview with parish priest?

Who will lead the children's formal catechesis?

- school (in addition to the HIA[1] programme)?
- parish (in addition to the school HIA programme)? e.g. weekly/monthly sessions?
- family (in addition to the school HIA programme)?
- parish in addition to the basic programme (WWM[2])?

Working with parents
   a. With what aim

- explaining the child's preparation?
- involving the parents in the child's preparation?
- helping parents as parents?
- deepening understanding and faith?

1. HIA *Here I Am,* Ann Byrne, Chris Malone *et al*, HarperCollins, 1992
2. WWM *Walk With Me,* Anne White, McCrimmons Publishing Co Ltd, 1996

b. Led by

- school staff?
- parish priest?
- parish team?

c. Where

- school?
- parish centre?
- church?
- home?

d. When

- evenings?
- daytime?

Involvement in community liturgical celebrations

- in school?
- at parish Sunday Mass?
- with parish other than Sunday Mass?

Involvement of parish community

- in liturgical celebrations?
- as prayer sponsors/friends?
- as catechists?

Celebration of First Holy Communion

- as one large group?
- smaller groupings?
- families individually?
- at parish Sunday Mass?
- at a special Mass?

2. Planning the Timetable

Decide when the sacrament is to be celebrated and then plan your timetable. This proposed outline is intended to be adapted.

The timing will be affected by Holy Week and Easter as well as how the celebration of First Holy Communion is planned, e.g. over one, two or a number of weekends.

December/early January	Session 1 (Introduction)
January	Session 2
February	Session 3
March	Session 4
April/May	Session 5
May	Celebration(s) of First Holy Communion
June	Final session/evaluation/celebration

Some variations

a. The parents' sessions are offered on a weekly basis *prior* to the commencement of the children's preparation, with a 'practicalities' session shortly before the celebration of the sacrament.

Advantages

Parents get to know one another more quickly, names are remembered, trust and friendships build up and the discussion is subsequently entered into more deeply. Parents have an overview of the sacrament before the children's preparation begins.

Disadvantages

It may be hard to maintain contact with parents if they don't meet on a monthly basis. However, Family Links may overcome this disadvantage.

b. The first and last sessions are held as one large gathering, the 'middle' sessions are held in smaller, neighbourhood groups.

Advantages

Where there are large numbers involved, or where people are travelling from distances, this may lead to more personal communications.

Disadvantages

The sense of parish identity being developed through the whole group meeting together doesn't happen as quickly when the whole group is not meeting regularly – with careful organisation this is not insurmountable!

c. Offering a choice of times when parents can come to a session, e.g. evening or the following morning – perhaps making provision at the morning session for the presence of toddlers.

Advantages

It helps parents to realise you understand the realities of life!

Disadvantages

More time and effort is required from the team. With planning, this is not insurmountable.

3. Themes

It is intended that the themes are adapted according to the particular group of parents. Parishes may prefer to select their own titles. In general it brings a greater coherence to the programme if these correlate with the themes of the children's sessions and the celebrations.

First Holy Communion

Session 1.	'Come and see' Introduction and Enrolment
Session 2.	'Do this in memory of me' Exploring the Mass – What Is It About?
Session 3.	'Speak, Lord, your servant is listening' Exploring the Mass – the Liturgy of the Word
Session 4.	'My soul proclaims the greatness of the Lord' Exploring the Mass – the Liturgy of the Eucharist
Session 5.	'Let your light shine' Exploring the Mass – Going Out from Mass

4. Including Parishioners with Disabilities

Integration means placing the individual within the desired group/community.

Inclusion entails being enabled to enter into relationship and gradually acquire an accepted and valued role so that there is a sense of mutuality with the group/community.

Why include parishioners with disabilities? This is what the Gospel calls us to do.

Paul reminds us that those who seem to be the weakest are the indispensable ones (1 Corinthians 12:22).

If we exclude people with disabilities, we lose a great richness and diversity and are the poorer. We deprive the whole Christian community of part of its natural growth in building up the Body of Christ.

We are a pro-life Church and must show this by our commitment to welcome into our community people with disabilities, from the developing foetus to the child, the adult and the elderly person, with all that person's experiences and gifts.

> Respect for the human person considers the other 'another self'. It pre-supposes respect for the fundamental rights that flow from the intrinsic dignity of the person.
>
> *Catechism of the Catholic Church*, para. 1944
> Geoffrey Chapman, 1995

In welcoming people we enter into relationship with them. Learning to relate and to communicate with each other is an essential part of living, of loving and of entering into a relationship with God.

Parents, whether or not their children attend special schools, rightly hope they will be seen as part of the Christian community. Finding ways of accomplishing this often requires extra thought and planning. Welcoming and *including* disabled children and adults does not always mean full participation in the parish programmes for catechetics – sometimes it does. There are many ways of positively including people and celebrating together. Our responsibility is to find those ways and ensure that reception of a particular sacrament marks a deepening of inclusion in the Church and parish.

© Rosemary McCloskey and June Edwards
St Joseph's Pastoral Centre, Diocese of Westminster

Essential reading
Valuing Difference: People with Disabilities in the Life and Mission of the Church, The Bishops' Conference of England and Wales, Department for Catholic Education and Formation, 1998.

You might find it helpful to read:

General Directory for Catechesis, paragraphs 37, 42, 133, Catholic Truth Society, 1997.

Sharing our Faith – Involving People with Learning and Communication Difficulties in the Spiritual Life of the Parish, June Edwards. Matthew James Publishing Ltd, 1997.

Sharing our Faith – Celebrating First Eucharist, June Edwards. Matthew James Publishing Ltd, 1997.

Sharing our Faith – Celebrating Confirmation, June Edwards. Matthew James Publishing Ltd, 1997.

Developmental Disabilities and Sacramental Access, ed. Edward Foley. In particular, Chapter 5, 'Canonical Rights to the Sacraments', John Huels. The Liturgical Press, Minnesota, 1994.

5. Journeying with Parents – preparing a foundation

Preparing to celebrate First Holy Communion can be very important for parents in renewing and deepening their own faith.

To prepare for this some schools/parishes invite parents to come together for a series of gatherings in the first or second year of their child's schooling

- to develop friendships
- to build up community
- to give experience of working in groups
- to give the opportunity to share questions that are of concern.

Such an experience reduces the shyness and awkwardness that can dominate the early sessions of the preparation for first sacraments.

Useful resources

Noughts to Sixes Parenting Programme, M. and T. Quinn, Family Caring Trust, 1995 (for meetings with parents of young children)

Moments that Matter. Book 1: Starting School, Pastoral Formation Department, Archdiocese of Liverpool, Rejoice Publications, 1995.

'Coffee and chat' groups hosted by a catechist/parishioner with an informal agenda arising from topics parents want to discuss.

Helpful Hints for the Catechist _____

1. The Team

Gathering the team

The 'team' involves all those taking responsibility for a different part of the meeting. It could include any/all of the following. Adapt the team according to your resources.

- Priest: is he pastor? spiritual guide? visitor to each family? catechist? resource? The priest's role on the team requires clarification.

- Programme co-ordinator: to co-ordinate the overall programme, ensuring the appropriate partnership of home, school and parish, as well as the various team members.

- Catechist: to work with the parents, leading into and developing the theme.

- Candidates' teacher/catechist: to explain to parents what the preparation of the children involves and how the parents can support this at home.

- Parent: to share ways of living the theme in the family setting.

- Liturgy Link: explaining what is happening in the proposed liturgy and inviting the parents' participation.

- Family Link: welcoming the parents, helping with refreshments.

Once the team is gathered

Discuss together

- What formation and preparation have our team had?
- What on-going support do members need/want?

Weak and Wobbly Hearts

Christian action is done by you and me, ordinary people with weak and wobbly hearts who do not have the security of trained skills, etc. I think Christian action and the promotion of the Kingdom is done by those who are afraid of what people will say, who are a bit cowardly, who are a bit diffident about standing up in public, do not have the security of plenty of practice and experience, can be capsized by failure, hurt by remarks, hurt by being ignored; find themselves reacting jealously when they do not want to, are overcome by despair, yet go on loving and trusting. It is the weak and wobbly hearts that Christ chooses, as he chose Peter, James, John, Thomas – all the disciples. They were not the high fliers of Galilee or Judaea, they were the ordinary folk, capable of love.

Letting Go in Love, Fr John Dalrymple
Darton, Longman & Todd, 1986

Pause for thought
*Have **you** ever felt like this?*

Questions for the team

Questions for the team to consider when meeting to plan the programme, focusing on *this* group of parents:

1. What are our hopes/concerns as we begin this programme?

2. How as a team do we work? Who does what? What time? How often will we meet? Where?

3. Who is the leader? Who do parents see as the leader? What's the role of the parish priest, head teacher, catechist – each member of the team?

4. Why are the parents gathering?

5. What are their expectations?

6. What commitment are we expecting from participants? How will this be agreed?

7. What timing, balance, plan of the session is most appropriate for this group?

8. How do we build relationships with the group members?

9. Are there different personalities: angry? shy? hurt? How do we respond to them?

10. Are there undercurrents? hidden agenda?

11. What is the previous experience history of the group? For example, have they been involved in a parenting programme? other sacramental programmes?

12. What is the starting point for this group? For example, white dresses(!), divorce/ remarriage? What are the questions *this group of parents* wants to discuss? How will the team respond?

13. Are there other questions/issues team members want to raise?

You might find it helpful to read:

The Sign We Give, Bishops' Conference of England and Wales, Matthew James Publishing Ltd, 1995.

Journeying together in faith

Catechesis is about accompanying others on their faith journey as they seek to deepen their relationship with Christ. You have the privilege of walking with others for a few months of their life-long journey.

The starting point is the present stage of others: start from where they are.

Be sensitive to the feelings of the parents – for many this may be their first experience of adult catechesis and of working in groups.

If this is the first contact of some parents with the Church since their child's baptism, some of their questions/comments may be:

- I can't go to Communion.
  I've been married twice.
  What's the point of coming to Mass?

- I've not been married in Church.

- I'm divorced.
  I feel I've no place in the Church.

- I'm not a Catholic, what's it all about?

- I've not been to Church for years.
  It's all changed; it doesn't make sense any more.

In your team's preparation, discuss together, particularly with the parish priest, how you will respond to these pastoral needs if they surface.

If, at the introductory meeting, a series of questions emerge, and you feel it is appropriate to base the subsequent sessions on these, do so! Hopefully the resources provided will help you to plan such sessions.

Catechesis is about sharing faith. Be ready to *listen* as well as to talk.

Remember – you too are invited to journey!

You might find it helpful to read:
Our Faith Story, A. P. Purnell, Collins, 1985.

Standing in another's shoes – an initial reflection for team members

Catechesis invites us to journey in faith with another. Sometimes it can be helpful when we start with a new group to pause, step out of our own shoes and attempt to stand in the shoes of those with whom we hope to journey, to glimpse life from their perspective. Take time to do the following exercise.

Think of a parent you know who wants his/her child to celebrate First Holy Communion.

Stand in that person's shoes. Spend a few moments reflecting personally on the following:

Describe, using the word 'I', the realities of life, for instance their family, domestic, social, financial, spiritual situation.

In that person's shoes, try to explore:
• What bothers me most?
• What gives me life?
• What do I hope for?
• What destroys or takes away my life?
• What do I see when I look at the Church?
• What might the Church have to offer me?
• What am I expecting from the Church for my child as we prepare to celebrate this sacrament?

As you step back into your own shoes, what insights have you gained from this reflection? Take time to write these down. Share them with the team. As you listen to one another, be aware of how your reflections might affect your planning.

(Adapted with permission from an exercise used by Pat Jones)

2. The Session in Outline

Framework of a session

Apart from the introductory session, for which a particular framework is suggested, the material for each session is divided into the following sections:

1. Preparing the session
2. Welcome and introduction
3. Leading into the theme: describe and explore
4. Developing the theme: listen
5. Reflecting on the theme: reflect and relate to life
6. Living the theme
7. Celebrating the theme
8. Praying the theme
9. Closing the meeting.

Length of session: 1 hour 30 minutes.

NB: Don't forget to plan when you are going to have refreshments.

The content offered is primarily adult catechesis, drawing considerably on the scriptures. In the structure suggested, time is allocated towards the end of each session for the group to reflect on how, as parents, in the light of all that has been shared, they will be able to help their children to grow in faith. You may prefer to reverse the order by beginning the session with the practical issues relating to parents/ parenting and then focus on the catechetical dimension.

At some stage during the course of the sessions it will obviously be necessary to deal with all the practicalities concerning the celebration of First Holy Communion – the time for this will vary according to the local situation. Decide when and where it fits in with *your* sessions and plan accordingly.

For each session for First Holy Communion suggestions for a 'Family Sheet' are given. It is anticipated that this will be taken home. Please adapt it! (See, for instance, the two pages following on page 53.)

Page 1. Introducing the theme

Page 2. Developing the theme

Page 3. Suggestions for living and celebrating the theme at home, at Mass.
(Space is allocated for notes concerning what the children are asked to complete in their workbooks this month.)

Page 4. Suggestions for prayer
(Space is allocated for writing in dates for the diary.)

The Family Sheet alone could be used with parents as a discussion starter where preparation is taking place more informally.

The sections of the session

The Pastoral Cycle – a way of working

Leading into the theme   DESCRIBE AND EXPLORE
Developing the theme   LISTEN
Reflecting on the theme   REFLECT AND RELATE TO LIFE
Celebrating the theme   PRAY AND CELEBRATE

This is based on a process, a methodology generally known as the 'Pastoral Cycle'.

For some, it is recognised in the more familiar form of SEE, JUDGE, ACT. This is a model created by the Belgian priest Joseph Cardign and used in his work with Young Christian Workers in the period between the two world wars. It remains in use in YCW and YCS work today.

The Pastoral Cycle was developed from this model by liberation theologians. We see it strongly reflected in the work of Paulo Freire and Juan Luis Segundo. It is a methodology for LIFE.

- It invites those involved to stand back and see what is happening, to NAME and DESCRIBE and then to EXPLORE it – asking the who/what/why questions. A clearer picture of why things are as they are can emerge at this stage.
- The next stage is to LISTEN to appropriate scripture, the Church's tradition, teachings, doctrine, history, experience – so broadening the vision.
- This listening is followed by REFLECTION leading to APPROPRIATION – that is, making it part of *my* life.
- Through this reflective process, change becomes possible, resulting in ACTION.
- This shared experience is a cause for CELEBRATION.

In more recent years, the Pastoral Cycle has become the accepted process for Religious Education and catechesis. It reflects catechetical principles.

A more detailed study of the Pastoral Cycle illustrates that it reflects the movement in the Emmaus story (Luke 24) of the disciples coming to a deeper faith in the Lord, and, in fact, models the way the Lord journeyed with the two disciples.

In working with adults, it is a recommended approach because

- it recognises, respects and takes seriously their life experience
- it recognises the importance of the Church's tradition – scripture, teachings, doctrine – informing that experience
- it invites change, action, growth, development and conversion, essential for Christian discipleship and mission in the world today.

You might find it helpful to read:

Christian Religious Education, Thomas Groome. Harper & Row, 1980.

Let's Do Theology, Laurie Green. Mowbray, 1990.

Structure of the session

Welcome and introduction

Many parents have rushed to arrive in time for the session. They come from having sorted out meals, children, bedtime, baby-sitters – all that goes on in a household in the early evenings. Their minds may well still be with all that was going on in the house before they left, wondering if the children are all right, what *did* happen in that last ten minutes of *Coronation Street*, etc., etc! To 're-orientate' themselves suddenly into the First Sacraments preparation may take a few minutes. Much will have happened in the lives of people since the last session, so a sensitive introduction can help people settle into the session more quickly. For example, if there has been a parish liturgy for the group since the last session, reference to it at this point can help to focus thoughts; or comment could be invited on how they managed with the suggestions for 'living the theme'. Drawing attention to the 'focal point' can be a way of opening up this session's theme.

Consider what opening prayer is appropriate.

Team member   Programme co-ordinator
Time allocation   5 minutes

Leading into the theme: describe and explore

The purpose of this part of the session is to enable participants to get in touch with their own experience of the particular theme, their 'story'. Various suggestions/ worksheets are given as ways of leading into each theme. It is for the catechist to select what would be most appropriate for their group, and to introduce it as a spoken/written task.

Rather than organise small group discussion (which involves moving chairs and disturbing people just as they have settled), the suggestion at this point is that once people have had the chance for quiet reflection, they are then invited to 'buzz' (share thoughts) with those on either side. An opportunity for group discussion will be given later.

The feedback can be recorded on the flipchart and provide the lead into the next part of the session.

- An alternative to the flipchart: pieces of wallpaper attached to the wall, pattern side against the wall.

- It is useful to keep a supply of pens and 'rest boards' for using with worksheets. ('rest boards'– pieces of thick card slightly bigger than the worksheets made from cardboard boxes and covered with wallpaper.)

Team member   Catechist
Time allocation   5-10 minutes, depending on the task.

Developing the theme: listen

During this part of the session time is given for 'input', for sharing scripture, the Church's story, teaching and traditions. For many adults this is their first experience of such an opportunity since leaving school. A variety of ways of presentation can be used – talks, video, fact sheet, slides with text, film strip, passages from the Bible or other suitable texts to name but some. Diocesan RE centres provide useful resources. New material is constantly being published – it is as well for the catechist to be alerted to this. In the notes provided, resources are suggested, *please adapt!* Particular references from the scriptures are given. For many adults, to present the theme from this scriptural dimension is to open up a whole new world – yet one that is vital for those striving to live a Christian, Gospel-centred life.

It is anticipated that the catechist, having decided on which aspect of the theme they are going to take, will prepare a presentation from the resources available according to the needs of the group.

Team member   Catechist
Time allocation   10 minutes

Reflecting on the theme: reflect and relate to life

Suggested questions based on the theme are offered – adapt them accordingly. The feedback from each group will allow the opportunity for further input if necessary, as well as allowing individuals to begin to relate all that they have heard to their *own* lives. Points to develop at the next session may emerge from this discussion. Be alert!

Team member   Catechist
Time allocation   Group work, 15 minutes
                              General feedback, 15-20 minutes

Living the theme

a. The family at home

Suggestions are given on each 'Family Sheet' for ways for parents to develop the theme at home. In addition there may be requests from the candidate's teacher/catechist for parents to follow through particular work. This is a useful time to share these with the parents and to offer them encouragement.

b. The family at Mass

Suggestions are given on the 'Family Sheet' to enable parents to help to focus their child's attention at Mass, gradually leading to greater participation in the Eucharist.

Team member   Teacher/catechist/parent
Time allocation   10 minutes

Celebrating the theme

Some parishes integrate regular liturgies into their programme of preparation. It is helpful if parents are given the necessary details, especially if they are going to be invited to be involved in a particular way. Parents who are unfamiliar with the Mass can find the liturgies somewhat bemusing and consequently find it hard to participate.

Suggestions for an Enrolment Service for First Holy Communion are given in Part 2.

Team member   Priest/catechist/Liturgy Link
Time allocation   5 minutes

Praying the theme

Resources are provided for a short period of prayer/meditation to draw the session to a close. In this busy, noisy and cluttered life, many parents really appreciate the opportunity for silence and prayer that such meditation can offer. To make use of the variety of ways of praying suggested in the resources means the catechist may be leading individuals to discover new ways of praying: the heart of catechesis, of which the aim is to put people 'not only in touch but in communion, in intimacy with Jesus Christ' (*Catechesi Tradendae*, para. 5).

Team member   Programme co-ordinator/catechist/priest
Time allocation   5-7 minutes

Closing the meeting

Allow time for any final comments, such as queries, notices to be given, etc. Try to ensure parents are not going home confused and upset. Thank the parents for coming. Make sure the team is available if individual parents need to chat.

Team member   Programme co-ordinator

After the meeting

The team

- tidies the room
- shares initial comments about the meeting
- decides/confirms who will follow through with any parents missing from the meeting
- checks each member has the details of the date, time and venue for the next meeting.

3. Preparation

Practical preparation – setting the scene

Room preparation

- What is the layout of the room?
- How are the chairs arranged – do they suggest sharing/discussion (semi-circle) or instruction (straight lines facing the speaker's desk)?
- Is the team separated from the parents by the barrier of a big desk, or are they a part of the circle?
- What focal point suggests the theme of the session?
- What, in the arrangement, decoration and atmosphere of the room is going to encourage parents to enjoy and participate in the session?
- Are the necessary facilities easily available and clearly marked?
- Are the heating and lighting adequate?
- Can the flipchart be seen?

Welcome and hospitality

- Who greets the parents?
- Are name badges worn?
- How is a record of attendance kept? (It can be helpful to write the name of the child or family on the Family Sheet and place these on a table for the parents to collect as they arrive. Those left at the end of the evening indicate the absentees.)
- When are refreshments to be given? Served by whom?

Leadership

- Is it sensitive? listening? informed? respectful? competent?

Session

- Are the required materials at hand?
- How visual are the visual aids?
- How audible are audio aids?
- How well-presented are the handouts? Do they respect the literacy level of the group? Meet the needs of any illiterate adults?
- Is it planned to involve everyone? How?

In the notes for each session a 'Planning Sheet' is offered to help with the preparation.

Reminders for a first session

• What welcome and hospitality is there?

• What does the arrangement of the room say to people?

• What are people feeling, coming for the first time?

• Do we put people off by asking them to do things before they are ready to do so?

• Do we make people feel inadequate by the way we speak, do things?

• Do we frighten people by giving them pens, papers as soon as they walk through the door?

• Are we aware of the previous experiences of group members?

• Do people know what is happening? Tonight? In the following sessions?

• What fun and enjoyment is there?

• What are we going to do that sends people home feeling affirmed and valued? (And making them look forward to coming back?)

• What would *you* add to this list?

In working with people, do not try to call them back to where they were, and do not try to call them to where you are, as beautiful as that place might seem to you. You must have the courage to go with them to a place that neither you nor they have been before.

Christianity Rediscovered, Vincent Donovan
SCM Press, 1978

Presenting the theme – an overview

Leading into the theme

Plan how you will encourage the participants to name and reflect on their experience of the theme/topic.

Developing the theme

Prepare 'input' from the richness of the scriptures, the Church's tradition and teachings. (Appropriate presentation, with variation over a number of sessions, is vital.)

Reflecting on the theme

Offer suitable questions/topics for discussion and sharing, arising from the 'input' for small groups.

Allow time for feedback from the whole group.

Living the theme

Relate the theme to everyday living, especially family life.

Share together ways in which it can be
a. lived at home
b. linked in with the celebration of the Eucharist.

Celebrating the theme

Explain what liturgy is planned for the group, and how each family is invited to participate.

Praying the theme

Choose an appropriate way of praying with which to end the session.

NB: When will refreshments be served?

Planning a focal point

Focal points, well prepared, can speak to the parts of us that words fail to reach.

As you plan your session, discuss together what visual presentation of the theme you can offer using pictures? objects? fabrics? colour? icons? candles? incense?

Is it a different focal point each session or one built up over the series of sessions, reflecting their progression?

Be simple!   Be creative!

Be thoughtful!   Be bold!

Presenting the theme – preparing yourself

Spend time reflecting on the theme.
Let it buzz around *your* head for some days before the meeting.
Begin to get in touch with how it relates to *your* experience.
How is it part of *your* life?

Use the theme as a basis for your prayer.

Recall to mind your group.
It is these whom you are accompanying on their faith journey.

Summarise in a sentence the content of the theme you hope to present.

From your experience:
• What are the most successful ways of stimulating the parents' participation and involvement?

• What kind of material and presentation is most appropriate for them?

Using the resources provided:
• Plan how you will 'set the scene' (see page 33).

• Plan how to lead into the theme.
  Select from the material offered.
  Interest is maintained if you can vary the approach from meeting to meeting.

• Prepare your 'input'.
  What story from everyday life are you going to use to introduce it?
  Reflect on the resources offered.
  What appropriate passages from scripture could you use?
  What particular parts from the Church's Tradition are you going to share?

Prepare the questions to stimulate reflection and discussion.
• Are those offered in the resources suitable for your group?

Choose a closing meditation/prayer to reflect the theme.
• Are the resources offered appropriate?

After the meeting, with the whole team if possible, reflect on all that happened:
• What do we need to carry through to the next session?
• What would you change in your approach next time?

It is valuable for the whole team to discuss these points.

4. The Session in Practice

Leading a session

- Make sure the meeting room is warm, well-lit and comfortable.

- Welcome each person.

- Use people's names when speaking with them.

- Clarify the purpose of the session. Confirm this is agreed and accepted by all.

- Agree the 'boundaries', e.g. all that is spoken remains confidential, only one person speaks at a time so that all can hear . . .

- Affirm each contribution made.

- Invite participation of *all* members.

- Be alert for the less confident, less articulate members.

- Foster acceptance of individual opinions/feelings.

- Use your gift of humour!

- Befriend silence.

- Ensure the set task is achieved – as far as possible.

- Finally, thank the group for their participation.

Working with groups

Begin by

- inviting people to introduce themselves. This helps to build friendship in the group, it can be easier to talk with friends rather than strangers.

Explain

- All that is shared in groups is confidential.
- There are no 'First Prizes'! It is parents' thoughts and comments that are being invited, rather than knowledge being tested.
- The invitation is to *listen* rather than argue or debate.
- When worksheets are filled in, these are for the individual's eyes only.
- No one else will be looking at them: it does not matter how good or bad a person's spelling or drawing may be, no one else will see the worksheet.

Finally

- Ask the group to appoint a spokesperson to give any feedback.

Feedback

- Take the feedback from each group in turn before starting any general discussion.
- Record it on the flipchart. This helps the group to 'own' it.
- Once all the feedback is recorded:
  - glance over it
  - decide which points you will leave until next time – with the agreement of the group
  - decide which points you will deal with immediately – and do so.
- Try to draw things together on a positive note.

Remember

- Be sensitive! What *you* have offered in the 'input' may be new to some parents.
- A helpful way of stimulating group participation is to invite:
  - individual reflection
  - then sharing in twos
  - followed by sharing in the small group.

You might find it helpful to read:
Working with Groups, CAFOD, 1986.

Using scripture

The Word of God is something alive and active: it cuts like any double-edged sword but more finely (Hebrews 4:12).

- The way we pick up, hold, reverence the Bible, all speak of the importance we give the Word.

- The Hebrew scriptures are part of our shared tradition with the Jewish people and so should be treated with respect for their tradition as well.

- If appropriate, set the passage in context. Scripture is the Word of God and that Word is spoken to us today. However, it was written at a particular historical period and some awareness of the background can help us to deepen and enrich our interpretation and understanding of God's Word.

- Invite listeners to prepare themselves to hear the Word before it is proclaimed.

- Allow the Word to convey its own message to the listener.

- Invite listeners to share what they have heard, so enriching one another.

- Follow the listening and shared reflection with a pause for quiet prayer, allowing individuals time to make their own response to the Word spoken.

You might find it helpful to read:

Focus on the Bible, H. J. Richards, Kevin Mayhew Ltd, 1989.

Not Counting Women and Children, Megan McKenna, Orbis Books, 1994.

Gospel Light, John Shea, The Crossword Publishing Co, 1998.

Praying the theme

- Over the series of sessions, vary the type of prayer experience offered. People pray in different ways. Some are particularly grateful for having new ways of prayer offered to them.

- Create an atmosphere for prayer,
  e.g. light a candle, play quiet music, turn down the lighting.

- Draw attention to the focal point,
  e.g. icon, Bible, candle, screen if slides are to be used.

- *Invite* the group to participate – not all will be in the mood for praying. Some may prefer to sit quietly. Respect this.

- Give a brief outline of what is involved.

- Lead into the prayer from the discussion using the theme of the session.

- Prayer content – opening hymn/prayer – reading;
  pause for individual, then shared, reflection – invitation to share intercessions.

- Draw the prayer to an end in a definite way – with a hymn or blessing, for example:
  May the Lord bless you and keep you.
  May the Lord let his face shine on you
     and be gracious to you.
  May the Lord uncover his face to you
     and bring you peace.
  (Numbers 6:24-26)

- At some stage during the prayer, invite all the group to participate vocally, e.g. 'For all we have shared this evening we praise and thank the Father, praying, "Glory be to the Father . . . "' (said by all) or singing a simply worded hymn, e.g. 'Be still and know that I am God.'

Be adventurous!
- Use quiet music as a background to readings.
- Use slides to illustrate readings.
- Use taped songs that are familiar to the group so they can join in the refrain. These could be illustrated with one, or a series of slides.
- Use readings involving a number of voices (allow readers to prepare).
- Use silence!

You might find it helpful to read:

Helping Children to Pray, R. Cardwell, The Grail, 1981.

Biblical Prayers, L. Deiss, World Library Publications, 1976.

Starting Points, Sr Judith Russi SSMN, Geoffrey Chapman, 1991.

The Edge of Glory, David Adam, Triangle/SPCK, 1985.

Praying with Children, Jenny Pate, McCrimmons, 1995.

Reviewing Progress

1. Who has taken the *responsibility* for the sessions – school? parish? partnership of both?

2. Has the *main thrust* of the meetings been parenting? giving information? adult catechesis?

3. How were the *meetings organised* – one large group? small groups around the parish? individual families with a catechist?
    How appropriate was this?

4. How are families with children with *learning disabilities/special needs* included?

5. How are families with children *not attending the parish school* included?

6. What has been the involvement of the parish community?

7. What has been the place of *liturgy* during the preparation – parish Sunday Eucharist? parish non-Eucharistic service? school assembly? school Mass?

8. How successful have the *Family Links* been in establishing and maintaining contact with families?

9. What contact/*pastoral visiting* has there been with families with minimal participation in the programme?

10. What *networking* has taken place to share/develop additional resources?

11. What *follow-up* to the programme is planned? How will it be organised? By whom? When?

12. How will the children's/parents' involvement in the *parish Sunday liturgies* be continued?

13. Have *you* any other thoughts, queries, comments, suggestions . . . ?

PART 2
Resources for Eucharist

Introduction

This resource contains material for sessions with parents whose children are preparing to celebrate their First Holy Communion. They are prepared for catechists offering a parish-based programme of preparation in partnership with the school and family. It is envisaged that catechists will be drawing on other resources for the children's preparation, for the community involvement, the liturgies during the preparation and the celebration of First Holy Communion. Part 2, Resources for Eucharist, has been prepared for use in conjunction with Part 1, Guidelines for Catechists, essential background reading for making the best use of Part 2.

The material is offered in the form of five sessions:

Session 1. 'Come and see'
Introduction and Enrolment

Session 2. 'Do this in memory of me'
Exploring the Mass – What Is It About?

Session 3. 'Speak, Lord, your servant is listening'
Exploring the Mass – the Liturgy of the Word

Session 4. 'My soul proclaims the greatness of the Lord'
Exploring the Mass – the Liturgy of the Eucharist

Session 5. 'Let your light shine'
Exploring the Mass – Going Out from Mass

Session 1 may be omitted if the group has already enrolled.

Within each session, there are resources for inviting parents
- to listen to suggestions for supporting the work of their child's teacher/catechist
- to reflect on what they can do at home as their child's 'first teacher in the ways of faith'
- to deepen their own understanding of this sacrament
- to reflect on their own faith journey
- to pray together.

In addition there is:
- a passage for the catechists' personal reflection on the theme
- a planning sheet to help the catechists with their practical preparation
- a planning sheet for the closing prayer
- resources/suggestions for the catechists' presentation of the theme to parents
- a Family Sheet for parents to take home.

Please *adapt* the material according to the requirements of your group of parents.

Initial team preparation

This material is only a tool – and any tool is only as good as its operator! Part 1, Guidelines for Catechists, provides a background for using these resources, as well as an explanation about their structure and organisation.

Before starting work with parents:
- Read through Part 1.
- Share any reflections.
- Work through any queries or difficulties.
- Ensure all team members are happy with the basic structure and organisation suggested in Part 1.
- Discuss any adaptations you may need to make.
- Decide the roles and responsibilities of individual team members.
- Agree the programme timetable – dates, times and venue.

As well as your skill as catechists, it is your team's understanding of Eucharist that will influence how well you accompany parents. As you prepare yourselves, it is recommended that the team take time to reflect together on the following questions:
- What does Eucharist mean for us?
- What do we want to share about the Eucharist with the group of parents?

Essential background reading:
One Bread, One Body, Catholic Bishops' Conferences of England and Wales, Ireland and Scotland. Co-published by the Catholic Truth Society, London, and Veritas Publications, Dublin, 1998.

Programme Timetable

Parents' sessions

VENUE _____

TIMES
Start _____ Finish _____

DATES
Session 1 _____ Session 4 _____

Session 2 _____ Session 5 _____

Session 3 _____

Team planning meetings

VENUE _____

TIMES
Start _____ Finish _____

DATES
Session 1 _____ Session 4 _____

Session 2 _____ Session 5 _____

Session 3 _____ Session 6 (Evaluation) _____

Celebrations

VENUE _____

TIMES
Start _____ Finish _____

DATES
Celebration 1 _____ Celebration 4 _____

Celebration 2 _____ Celebration 5 _____

Celebration 3 _____

Children's meetings (For information to help with the planning)

DATES _____

Session 1. 'Come and see'

Introduction and Enrolment

General outline

If this is the first meeting, the emphasis could be on the social side so that the group begins to get to know one another. As people arrive, refreshments (coffee and cake or cheese and wine) could be served. If parents are not known by the team, it would be helpful if they were visited prior to the meeting by a Family Link, and then welcomed by that team member on arrival. Each team member could be responsible for 'hosting' a particular number of families, ensuring they have refreshments and are introduced to other parents. For those who are unfamiliar with official parish functions and premises this can be a daunting occasion. Where families have been visited and given a personal invitation to the meeting, the sense of community in the group can develop more easily.

Preparing the session
Focal point
Symbols/pictures reflecting the theme of the session,
e.g. bread and wine, Bible, First Holy Communion certificate, prayer book.

Welcome
Formally welcome the group, thank the parents for coming. Introduce the team, explaining the role of each member. Invite the parents to introduce themselves to those sitting on either side. Explain the plan of the evening.

Listening and inviting
1. Clarify 'First Communion' – in particular for the benefit of any non-Catholic parents. Invite the group to share memories, stories, experiences . . . hopes of what First Communion will mean for their child. Allow time for discussion.

2. Give an outline of the proposed programme, explaining what is proposed and *why*. (It would be helpful if this is on the Family Sheet.) The following points could be included:

- Why parents have been invited – refer to Pope John Paul's address to parents (printed on the Family Sheet).

- The influences on children growing in faith – the different yet complementary roles of home, school and parish (Useful resource: *Guidelines,* J Gallagher, Collins Liturgical Publications, 1986).

- What you are inviting parents to participate in over the coming months:
  – how the preparation will be based on themes – and why
  – the plan and the purpose of parents' meetings.

- The involvement of the school (perhaps one of the staff could do this?), the parents' role and the way school and parish are working together.
- The arrangement for the catechesis of children attending schools other than the parish school.
- The place of the liturgies/celebrations.
- The role of prayer friends/prayer sponsors, and how this will be organised.
- Family Links.
- The enrolment procedure.

3. Invite the group to form small groups.
   NB: Be sensitive! For some, it may be the first time that they are working in this way. Suggest:
   – each person introduces themselves to the group;
   – someone offers to be 'spokesperson' for the group.

Give out 'Parents' Questions' (page 56) and invite the group to:
   – share any hopes, fears, questions about the programme.
   – list any topics or particular questions (not on the worksheet) that they would like to discuss during the coming meetings.

4. Feedback
- Listen to what each group has to say.
- Some questions may be answered easily there and then by the team.
- List the questions for future discussion on the flipchart. Respond, explaining what different topics will be covered. (Keep this list. Bring it to each meeting. Tick off the appropriate questions as they are covered. By the end of the programme, they should all have been discussed.)
- Draw this discussion to a close. Lead into . . .

Invitation to enrol
Give out the enrolment forms (page 57), inviting parents to complete and return them if they wish their family to take part in the programme. Ensure enough time has been given for issues/questions to be raised.

Prayer
Using the resources, plan a closing prayer to reflect the theme of the session.

Closing the session
Thank the group for their participation.
Final words . . .

After the meeting
Tidying up and clarifying communication with families not represented at the meeting.

Team preparation
Session 1: Planning sheet

1. Preparing yourselves

Share together your reflections on 'Pause and reflect . . . '
Reread 'Reminders for a first session', sharing any comments (Guidelines page 34).

2. Preparing for Session 1

Date _____   Time _____

Venue _____   Theme _____

Areas of responsibility	Team member
Publicity/reminder to parents of the next meeting	_____
Setting the scene	_____
Focal point	_____
Refreshments	_____
Welcome and introduction	_____
Listening and inviting	_____
Invitation to enrol	_____
Closing the session	_____
After the session – tidying up	_____
Contacting absent parents	_____

Resources

Family Sheet: what adaptations?   _____

Worksheets/handouts to be duplicated _____

Page numbers: _____   _____

❑ Flipchart ❑ Felts ❑ Tape recorder   _____

 *Session 1: Planning prayer*

Focal point _____

Creating a mood of prayer

Lighting a candle   yes/no

Taped music   yes/no

Taped song   yes/no

Invitation to pray

led by _____

Opening song/prayer

led by _____

Reading   with/without music backing
             with/without slides

Pause for reflection   with/without invitation to reread passage
                        with/without invitation to pick out keywords/phrases

Invitation to share reflection

led by _____

Invitation to share intentions

led by _____

Closing words/song

led by _____

Session 1 – Pause and reflect

As you read the following passage, reflect on the titles that have the most meaning for you. Share these with the team.

THE EUCHARIST – A RICH HISTORY

When we come to Mass, we are coming to an event that has a history that takes us back to Jesus himself, and even before. The way we celebrate today is a far cry from the informal meal of the Last Supper, but our links are very real.

Scholars argue about whether the Last Supper was a Passover meal or not, but what we do know is that the atmosphere, context and prayers were rooted in the commemoration of that event, which brought Israel freedom from slavery and gave them a new identity as a nation – the Passover and Exodus. For Christians, the Last Supper links Jesus' dying to a new Exodus, the power of which, through his rising from the dead, is now offered to all people. He is the new Paschal Lamb – his death and outpouring of blood frees and saves us. The meal of that night makes the power of those events present now, gives us our identity as his disciples and strengthens us to be faithful.

The first Christians recognised the importance of doing what Jesus had commanded – 'Do this in memory of me'. They met daily, we are told *'for the breaking of bread'* (Acts 2:42). St Paul writing to the Corinthians warns the faithful about their behaviour at the Lord's Supper (which really was a meal), reminding them of what they were doing – *'proclaiming the death of the Lord'* (1 Corinthians 11:26). These are the earliest descriptions and titles for what we now know as the Mass. They express the earliest understanding of what the Mass meant to the Church. 'Breaking of the Bread' speaks about a sharing, a oneness in Christ, symbolised by the one loaf broken and shared. The Lord's Supper reminds us of the meal dimension, perhaps forgotten in our ritual in recent centuries but now rediscovered and expressed as we gather round the table and receive food and drink.

Other titles that were given to this meal of identity were *Eucharist, Anamnesis,* and *Communion*. These words survive within the Christian tradition today, each with their own perspective and stress, but each enriching the others. The word *Eucharist* means thanksgiving. After all, that was central to the four actions of Jesus – 'he took bread, *blessed* it, broke it and gave it to the disciples'. The Jewish blessing is an act of giving glory to God for his wonderful saving work. We now use this word to describe the whole action as well as the great blessing prayer that is central to the celebration. *Anamnesis* is a Greek word that means 'memorial' or 'calling to mind'. It is a biblical word that means more than just recalling an event. It includes the dynamic element, 'making the past event present'. So for the Jew, the Passover isn't merely a memory of a past event. Its saving power is present in the ritual each year. So for Christians, God's dynamic and powerful saving action in Jesus is made present at each Mass. This word also applies to a part of the Eucharistic prayer that is prayed by the priest.

The word *Communion* is another early name. As it implies, it speaks both about communion with the Lord and with one another. This word became an important way of describing the fellowship of the disciples as Church.

The word *Mass* with which we in the West are most familiar probably goes back to around the fifth century. As it implies, the word means 'sent' *(missa)*. At first it may have referred to the catechumens who were sent out before the liturgy of the Eucharist began, but then later it came to include the whole community 'sent' to live the Mass in the world.

As the Church grew and faced up to different cultures and philosophies, so her way of celebrating became influenced and moulded. More and more, the principal participants became the clerics, with the people gradually becoming ever more distant. The stress on the experience of a shared meal, the sense of community and the values implicit in the sharing of one loaf, became replaced by more hierarchical and cultic expression which have survived through the centuries to this day.

It is because of a renewed appreciation of our history that we have experienced the liturgical reforms of recent years that have changed the way in which the Mass is celebrated. The way we celebrate must always be intelligible to ourselves as well as faithful to Jesus' command. We celebrate a wonderful mystery and each age has its contribution to make in enabling us to deepen our understanding. The variety of names for this foundational and identity-giving ritual says much more about its richness. As inheritors of this rich tradition we are privileged to be entrusted with handing on our faith to the next generations.

Rev Peter Morgan

Family Sheet and Session notes/handouts follow.

'Come and see'

Introduction and Enrolment

Preparing to Celebrate Holy Communion

Dear parents of these children: your love for Christ has made this day possible. For you are your children's teachers in the ways of faith. By what you say and do, you show them the truths of our faith and the values of the Gospel. This is indeed not only a sacred duty, but a grace, a great privilege. Many other members of the Church share in this task, but the main responsibility for your children's religious formation rests upon your shoulders. So try to make your homes genuinely Christian. Help your children to grow and mature as Jesus did at Nazareth, 'in wisdom, in stature and in favour with God and men'. Allow no one to take advantage of their lack of experience and knowledge. As you share with them in their personal pilgrimage to God, may you always be united in prayer and worship and in humble love of God and his people.

The Pope Teaches – The Pope in Britain
Pope John Paul II
Catholic Truth Society, 1982

Family prayer

Before you begin to pray, quieten yourselves.

Listen to the words of God:

'I have called you by your name, you are mine.'

Say them again and again very quietly.

Prayer

Lord God,
you know each one of us by our own special name,
you know all my family,
you love us so much.
Thank you for wanting us to share your love.
We make our prayer through Jesus your Son.
Amen.

Parish Programme

When we gather together to celebrate Eucharist, we gather as the family of God

At home

- When you do things as a family, make a point of commenting on how enjoyable it is.

- Look through family photographs of your childhood – talk about the good times, and perhaps the sad times, you had with your family. The point to emphasise is that it is good to belong to a family.

At Mass

- As you come into church, explain to your child why we bless ourselves with holy water, as a reminder of our Baptism.

- Before Mass begins, point out to your child the baptismal font, where she/he was baptised, the tabernacle, where we keep the Bread of Life, the crucifix, the table which becomes the altar, and the stand (lectern), from where God's Word is proclaimed.

Dates for the diary

Next meeting

Parents' questions . . .

What do I have to do?

When is it?

How do they receive Communion?

Is there a party?

What will it cost?

Do we get photographs?

What happens if we miss the meetings?

Why are we having all these meetings?

Why isn't the school doing it?

What's it got to do with us?

Why is it in the parish?

How do you know when they are ready?

Why should we go to Mass?

How do we explain it?

I think my child is too young − has she got to do it? Can she wait?

Why are we changing names, like saying Eucharist instead of Mass?

Fasting − do we have to?

Can non-Catholics receive Communion?

Can I, as a lapsed Catholic, receive Communion?

Can a person who has been married twice receive Communion?

What happened to the Catechism?

How can I as a non-Catholic parent help?

Is what I'm telling my child the same as what school is telling her?

What should the children wear?

Parish of

_____

Preparing to Celebrate
The Sacrament of Holy Communion

CHILD'S NAME _____

ADDRESS _____

_____

TELEPHONE NUMBER _____

DATE OF BIRTH _____

PLACE AND DATE OF BAPTISM _____

I/We wish our child to be a part of the Parish Programme of Preparation for Holy Communion and will do our best to help and support

_____

SIGNED _____

DATE _____

FATHER'S NAME _____

RELIGION _____

MOTHER'S NAME _____

RELIGION _____

Please return this form to the Presbytery,
with a copy of the Baptism Certificate.

Enrolment of Candidates for First Sacraments

To be adapted
Renewal of Baptismal Promises: (Replacing the Creed)
All stand

Priest	Parents, before you present your children to the parish to be prepared for First Holy Communion, you are invited to witness to your faith, together with all here present, by renewing the promises of your baptism. Do you believe in God, the Father almighty, maker of heaven and earth?
All	We do.
Priest	Do you believe in Jesus Christ his only Son who became man for us?
All	We do.
Priest	Do you believe in the Holy Spirit who lives in our hearts?
All	We do.

The Priest addresses the families of the candidates, the rest of the congregation are invited to sit.

Priest	Dear parents, what is it you ask of God's Church for your child?
Parents	First Holy Communion.
Priest	Are you willing to do your best to help your child to prepare to celebrate First Holy Communion?
Parents	We are, with the help of God.

The Priest blesses the medals, then invites the candidates and their families to come forward. Each child brings her/his name card and offers it to the Priest who exchanges it for a medal, after addressing the candidate in these or similar words:

Priest	N . . . , do you want to get ready to receive your First Holy Communion?
Candidate	Yes, please!
Priest	N . . . , wear this medal as a sign of being in the preparation group in our parish. *Priest places medal around the neck of the candidate.*

The congregation could be invited to sing an appropriate hymn during this time.

The Liturgy continues with the Prayer of the Faithful.

After Mass, the name cards could be displayed in an appropriate part of the church for the rest of the time of the programme, inviting the congregation to pray for the candidates.

NB: If there is a large group of children, catechists could be invited to help with the distribution of the medals.

Session 2. 'Do this in memory of me'

Exploring the Mass – What Is It About?

General outline

Preparing the session
Focal point
Symbols/pictures reflecting the theme of the session, e.g. two tables representing the Liturgy of the Word with Bible, candle and Missal, the other representing the Liturgy of the Eucharist with bread and wine.

Welcome
Welcome the group. Opening prayer. Invite the parents to introduce themselves to the person sitting on either side. Introduce the team. Explain the plan of the evening (especially time for refreshments!). Invite parents to share any comments, reflections since the last meeting.

Leading into the theme

Developing the theme ————————> see 'Adults journeying in faith' (page 68)

Reflecting on the theme

Living the theme ———————————— see Family Sheet
At home

- Explain what the children are doing with their teacher/catechist and how parents can support this.
- Making Sunday special – practical suggestions.
- Family prayer.

At Mass

- Focus on the Gloria.

Looking ahead

- Practicalities concerning   the next children's session
                                   the next parents' meeting.

Celebrating the theme
Explain the next Liturgy – its purpose, what is being asked of the children and their families; practical planning.

Prayer
Using the resources, plan a closing prayer to reflect the theme of the session.

Closing the session
Thank the group for their participation.
Final words . . .

After the meeting
Tidying up and clarifying communication with families not represented at the meeting.

Team preparation
Session 2: Planning sheet

1. Reviewing the last meeting

Questions for reflection   what went well?
with what were you disappointed?
what do you want to do differently?

2. Preparing yourselves

Share together your reflections on 'Pause and reflect . . . '

3. Preparing for Session 2

Date _____ Time _____

Venue _____ Theme _____

Areas of responsibility	**Team member**
Publicity/reminder to parents of the next meeting	_____
Setting the scene	_____
Focal point	_____
Refreshments	_____
Welcome and introduction	_____
Leading into the theme	_____
Developing the theme	_____
Reflecting on the theme	_____
Living the theme	_____
Closing the session	_____
After the session – tidying up	_____
Contacting absent parents	_____

Resources

Family Sheet: what adaptations? _____

Worksheets/handouts to be duplicated _____

Page numbers: _____ _____

❑ Flipchart ❑ Felts ❑ Tape recorder _____

Session 2: Planning prayer

Focal point _____

Creating a mood of prayer

lighting a candle   yes/no

taped music   yes/no

taped song   yes/no

Invitation to pray

led by _____

Opening song/prayer

led by _____

Reading   with/without music backing

with/without slides

Pause for reflection   with/without invitation to reread passage

with/without invitation to pick out keywords/phrases

Invitation to share reflection

led by _____

Invitation to share intentions

led by _____

Closing words/song

led by _____

Session 2 – Pause and reflect

As you read and reflect on the following passage, you might reflect on the centrality of the Sunday Liturgy in your own life as well as your experience of the parish Sunday Liturgy.

THE CELEBRATION OF SUNDAY

The Centrality of Sunday

'Whenever the community gathers to celebrate the Eucharist, it announces the death and resurrection of the Lord, in the hope of his glorious return. The supreme manifestation of this is the Sunday Assembly' *(Congregation for Rites, Instruction on the Worship of the Eucharistic Mystery, Eucharisticum Mysterium, Flannery, vol. I).* Gathering on Sunday for the celebration of the Eucharist has been an enduring characteristic and hallmark of the life of the Church. From the very beginning of Christendom, Sunday and the eucharistic celebration have been inseparable. Participation in the Sunday Eucharist was regarded as the hallmark and authentication of being a Christian. The Lord's Day and the Lord's Supper went hand in hand. Christians assembled for Sunday Eucharist not out of a sense of obligation but rather out of an inner conviction and a deeply felt spiritual need to share in the life of the risen Christ. This became real when they met together to relive what he had said and done. Sunday was primarily the commemoration and memorial of the resurrection. It was the 'original feast day', a kind of weekly Easter. By absenting themselves Christians felt they were cutting themselves off from the very source of life itself, i.e. the risen Christ. But even more importantly, they were conscious of diminishing and weakening the very fabric of the Christian community. Their overriding conviction was 'lest any man diminish the Church by not assembling, and cause the Body of Christ to be short a member' *(Didascalia Apostolorum).* We must try to recover these ancient insights in order to celebrate Sunday more fittingly.

The Sunday Liturgy: a Barometer of Faith

The Sunday Liturgy is the celebration of the faith-life and charity of the parish community and for this reason the Catholic Church has always placed a high premium on participating in Sunday worship. In the mind of the Church, the Liturgy acts as a kind of barometer of faith and holiness. Traditionally the sacraments were often used as a gauge of faith. Today the parish Liturgy provides a coherent sign of its spiritual well-being. 'The Sunday Eucharist is the foundation and confirmation of all Christian practice. For this reason, the faithful are obliged to participate in the Eucharist on days of obligation, unless excused for a serious reason (for example, illness, the care of infants) or dispensed by their own pastor. Those who deliberately fail in this obligation commit a grave sin' *(Catechism of the Catholic Church,* n 2181).

Recent years have witnessed a decline in the number of people going to Church regularly. 'A common reason for dropping the practice of Sunday Mass is boredom with the service. In an age when entertainment is much sought after and professionally packaged, boring the congregation must be avoided' ('A Living Liturgy . . . Every Sunday?', T. Prior, in *Intercom,* September 1990). If a person's experience of

Sunday Eucharist is cold and uninspiring, the sense of community is weakened and the bonds of faith and love are diminished as a result. Consequently, no effort should be spared when it comes to preparing for and celebrating the Sunday Eucharist. It takes precedence over everything else a priest has to do in his parish during the week.

A Parish Pastoral Directory, ed.William Dalton, Columba Press, 1995

Family Sheet and Session notes/handouts follow.

'Do this in memory of me'

Preparing to Celebrate Holy Communion

On Sundays there is an assembly of all who live in towns or in the country, and the memoirs of the apostles or the writings of the prophets are read for as long as time allows. Then the reading is brought to an end, and the president delivers an address in which he admonishes and encourages us to imitate in our own lives the beautiful lessons we have heard read. Then we all stand together and pray. When we have finished the prayer as I have said, bread and wine and water are brought up; the president offers prayers and thanks-giving as best he can, and the people say 'Amen' as an expression of their agreement. Then follows the distribution of the food over which the prayer and thanksgiving have been recited: all present receive some of it, and the deacons carry some to those who are absent.

St Justin Martyr, c.150

Family prayer

Before you begin this prayer, quieten down.
Be still.
Ask God to help you to pray.
Listen to God's words to you:
    'You are precious in my eyes'.
Listen to God saying those words, over and over again to you.

Prayer

Lord God,
each one of us is precious in your eyes.
That is wonderful!
Thank you.
We love you.
We want to live in your love.
Please help us.
We praise and thank you.
Amen.

At home

- Help your child to realise that Sunday is a special day, the Lord's day, by making it special. Decide together what you will do in future to make Sunday special.
- Make a list of the events your family celebrates – perhaps you could make up a calendar of them. Talk about why each one is so special. (The list could include birthdays, anniversaries, holidays.)

At Mass

- Look through family photographs of special occasions.
- Each Sunday help the children to understand that coming to Mass can be a joyful celebration.
- We can show our joy by singing – encourage the children to join in the hymns by your singing too.
- Encourage them to join in the responses, particularly *'And also with you'*, at the beginning of Mass.
- Particular prayer to concentrate on – the *Gloria*.
- Continue to encourage them to join in the *'Our Father'* as well as the *Amens*.

Dates for the diary

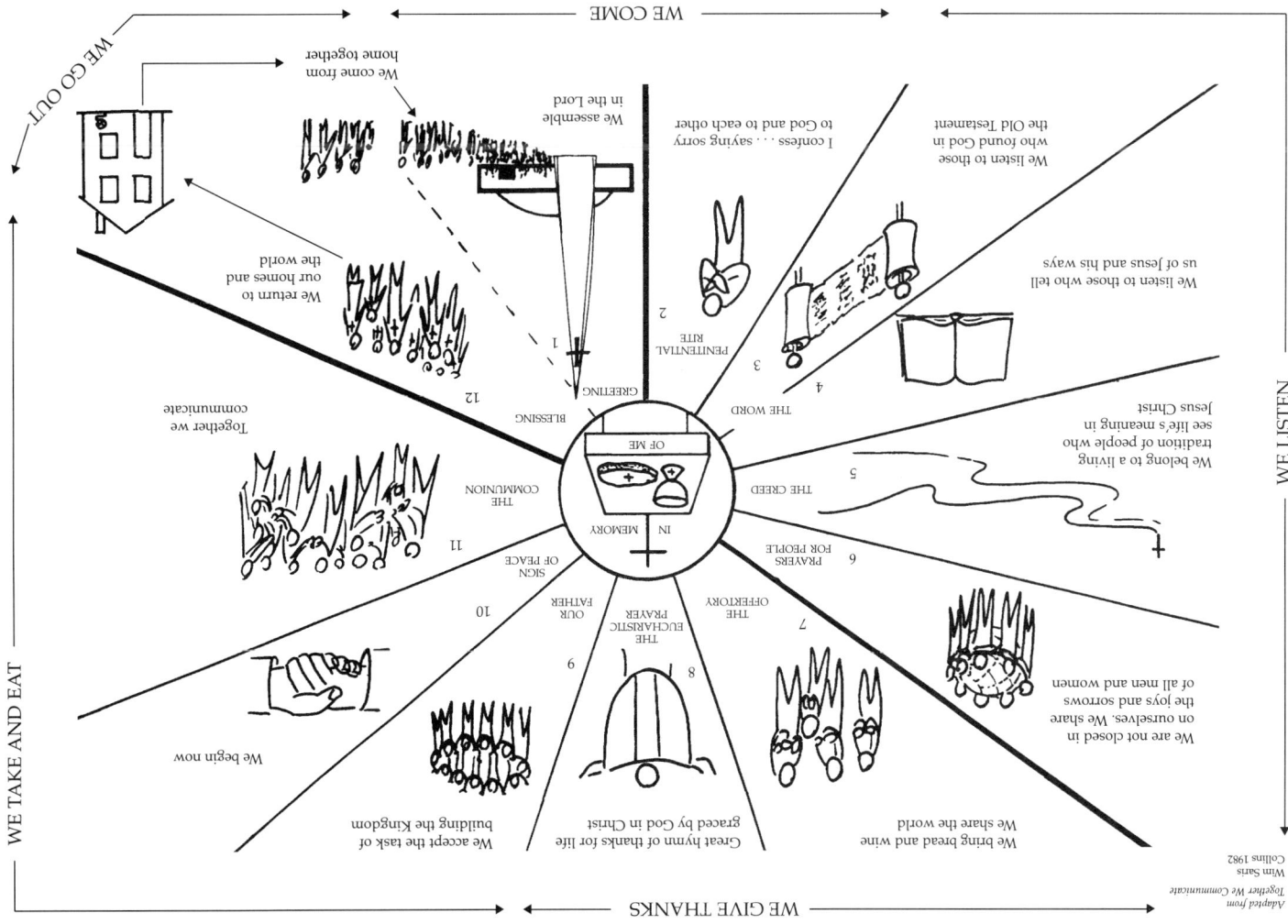

WE COME

WE GO OUT

WE LISTEN

WE TAKE AND EAT

WE GIVE THANKS

We come from home together

We assemble in the Lord

I confess . . . saying sorry to God and to each other

We listen to those who found God in the Old Testament

We listen to those who tell us of Jesus and his ways

We belong to a living tradition of people who see life's meaning in Jesus Christ

We are not closed in on ourselves. We share the joys and sorrows of all men and women

We bring bread and wine We share the world

Great hymn of thanks for life graced by God in Christ

We accept the task of building the Kingdom

We begin now

Together we communicate

We return to our homes and the world

1 GREETING

2

PENITENTIAL RITE

3

4 THE WORD

5 THE CREED

6 PRAYERS FOR PEOPLE

7 THE OFFERTORY

8 THE EUCHARISTIC PRAYER

9

10 OUR FATHER

SIGN OF PEACE

11 THE COMMUNION

12 BLESSING

IN MEMORY OF ME

Adapted from
Together We Communicate
Win Saris
Collins 1982

Adults journeying in faith – Catechists' notes

Exploring the Mass – What Is It About?
Introduce the theme – an overview of the Mass. Explain how this will be explored in greater detail in the following sessions.

A reflection:
The Prayer of the Holy Sacrifice of the Mass, John Shea (page 69), or the Justin Martyr passage (page70). The Family Sheet offers a shorter version.

Leading into the theme: describe and explore
- Invite the group to look with their neighbour at 'What's the Mass about?' (page 71). After a few moments, invite people to share their responses with the whole group.

  or

- 'Say it with flowers' (page 72). Put up an enlarged version on the flipchart. Ask the group to imagine that they are going to see someone. What are some of the things they might want to say as they present the flowers?

  Write down one statement on each flower. Suggest that this is done individually and quietly – no one is going to see their handwriting, spelling or answers! (Pens and 'rest boards' may need passing round.) Allow time for reflection (5 minutes?).

  Invite the group to 'buzz' with their neighbour, sharing/comparing some of their statements. Invite general feedback. Record the various 'sayings' on the flipchart: I'm sorry, I love you, Thank you . . .

  Draw out how similar these are to some of the things we come to do and say when celebrating Eucharist. Lead into . . .

Developing the theme: listen
A presentation exploring an overview of the Mass – what is it about? You may find the following resources helpful:
- Reflections on the Emmaus Story (pages 73-75)
- The Mass – Our Eucharistic Celebration (page 76)
- Illustration of the Mass (on Family Sheet).

Reflecting on the theme: reflect and relate to life
Invite the group to reflect in small groups on all they have heard. (Questions for discussion, page 78)

The Prayer of the Holy Sacrifice of the Mass

Those who do not believe in a Higher Harmony
will balk when told an accident crunched
in the parking lot at the very moment
the altar boy's nose began to bleed.
He bled on the surplice, the cassock,
the candle, the other altar boy,
and the priest's unlaced shoe
which bulgingly carried an Ace bandaged ankle.
The priest was stuffing a purificator up the
    boy's nose,
damming the blood into his eyeballs,
when the lector asked, 'How do you pronounce
E-l-i-s-h-a?' and the organist pounded
the entrance 'Praise to the Lord'.

They processed.
The bleeding, the halt, and the mute
unto the altar of God.

Saturday was late and liquored
and delivered God's people,
sunglassed and slumping, to the epilogue of
weekend life, the Gothic church.
They were not the community of liberal
    theology
nor the scrubbed inhabitants of film strips.
They were one endless face
and that face was asleep.

'May the grace of our Lord . . . '

A hungry pause for repentance.
A quick feast of sins.

The lector murdered the prophets once again
and bypassed the section where a certain
    E-l-i-s-h-a
was having prophetic truck with a widow.
The homily parlayed a fairly clear gospel
(you are either with me or against me)
into sentences of vacillation

and paragraphs of double-think.
The priest ran to the Creed for refuge
only to find a special creed was prepared
for this morning's liturgy by Mrs Zardek
'I believe in butterflies and the breath of . . .'

The courage of the president
of the liturgical assembly
drained into the boltholes
of communion rail days.

The offertory gifts never made it.
They were dropped by an elderly couple
('We never liked the new Mass anyway.')
who collided with a small but speedy child
whose high-heeled mother was in klicky-klack
    pursuit
and whose name was 'Rogercomeback'.

The consecration was consistent.
The priest lifted the host
and said 'This is my blood.'
Instantly aware of his eucharistic goof
but also momentarily in the grip of a bizarre
    logic
he changed the wine into Jesus' body.
Then
with his whole mind, heart, and soul
he genuflected
    – never to rise –
to a mystery which masks itself
as mistake
and a power which perfects itself
in weakness.

John Shea
The Hour of the Unexpected
Argus Publications, 1977

The Early Centuries

IN AD 150, ST JUSTIN WROTE THIS IN ROME:

No one may share in the Eucharist except those who believe in the truths of our teachings, and have been washed in the bath which confers forgiveness of sins and rebirth, and who live according to Christ's commands. For we do not receive this food as ordinary bread, and as ordinary drink . . . The apostles in their memoirs which are called Gospels, recorded that Jesus left them these instructions: he took bread, pronounced the prayer of thanksgiving and said: 'Do this in memorial of me. This is my Body.' In the same way he took the cup, pronounced the prayer of thanksgiving and said: 'This is my Blood', and shared it among them and no one else. From that time on we have always continued to remind one another of this. Those of us who are well provided help out any who are in need, and we meet together continually . . .

On Sundays there is an assembly of all who live in towns or in the country, and the memoirs of the apostles or the writings of the prophets are read for as long as time allows. Then the reading is brought to an end, and the president delivers an address in which he admonishes and encourages us to imitate in our own lives the beautiful lessons we have read. Then we all stand together and pray. When we have finished the prayer as I have said, bread and wine and water are brought up; the president offers prayers and thanksgiving as best he can, and the people say 'Amen' as an expression of their agreement. Then follows the distribution of the food over which the prayer and thanksgiving have been recited: all present receive some of it, and the deacons carry some to those who are absent. Those who are well provided for, if they wish to do so, contribute what each thinks fit; this is collected and left with the president, so that he can help the orphans, widows and the sick, and all who are in need for any reason, such as prisoners and visitors from abroad. So on Sunday we all come together. This is the first day, on which God transformed darkness and matter and made the world; the day on which Jesus rose from the dead.

What's the Mass about?

Look at the different responses . . .

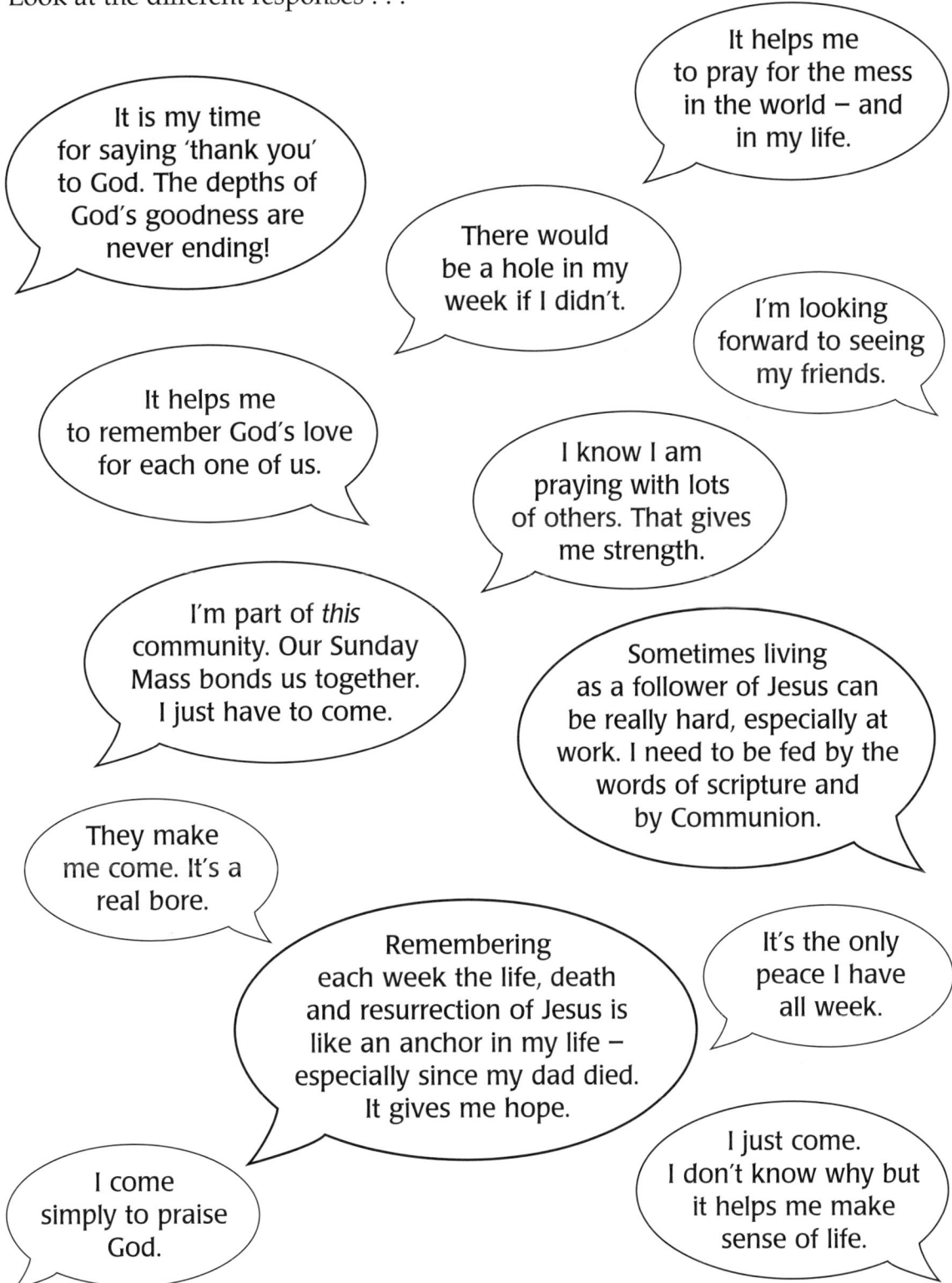

It helps me to pray for the mess in the world – and in my life.

It is my time for saying 'thank you' to God. The depths of God's goodness are never ending!

There would be a hole in my week if I didn't.

I'm looking forward to seeing my friends.

It helps me to remember God's love for each one of us.

I know I am praying with lots of others. That gives me strength.

I'm part of *this* community. Our Sunday Mass bonds us together. I just have to come.

Sometimes living as a follower of Jesus can be really hard, especially at work. I need to be fed by the words of scripture and by Communion.

They make me come. It's a real bore.

Remembering each week the life, death and resurrection of Jesus is like an anchor in my life – especially since my dad died. It gives me hope.

It's the only peace I have all week.

I come simply to praise God.

I just come. I don't know why but it helps me make sense of life.

1. Do any of the answers match your answer?

2. How would you like your child to answer?

What might we say?

Reflections on the Emmaus story and the Eucharist

Now on that same day two of them were going to a village called Emmaus, about seven miles from Jerusalem, and talking with each other about all these things that had happened. While they were talking and discussing, Jesus himself came near and went with them, but their eyes were kept from recognising him. And he said to them, 'What are you discussing with each other while you walk along?' They stood still, looking sad. Then one of them, whose name was Cleopas, answered him, 'Are you the only stranger in Jerusalem who does not know the things that have taken place there in these days?' He asked them, 'What things?' They replied, 'The things about Jesus of Nazareth, who was a prophet mighty in deed and word before God and all the people, and how our chief priests and leaders handed him over to be condemned to death and crucified him. But we had hoped that he was the one to redeem Israel. Yes, and besides all this, it is now the third day since these things took place. Moreover, some women of our group astounded us. They were at the tomb early this morning, and when they did not find his body there, they came back and told us that they had indeed seen a vision of angels who said that he was alive. Some of those who were with us went to the tomb and found it just as the women had said; but they did not see him.'

Penitential Rite: Lord, have mercy.
'Mourning our Losses'
LOSS: Luke 24:13-24

We come together in our brokenness before God, mourning our losses, Lord have mercy.

This is the cry of a people with a contrite heart, taking/accepting responsibility for the wrong we have caused or contributed to, for our part in the sinfulness of the world. Yet we make the prayer knowing, 'My grace is enough for you', because deep within us there is a yearning, a searching for love, unity and communion.

'It is only the broken soil that can receive the water and make the seed grow and bear fruit.'

In the Penitential Rite we acknowledge our brokenness.

The two on the road to Emmaus shared with the stranger all that was making them 'downcast', all their losses.

Then he said to them, 'Oh, how foolish you are, and how slow of heart to believe all that the prophets have declared! Was it not necessary that the Messiah should suffer these things and then enter into his glory?' Then beginning with Moses and all the prophets, he interpreted to them the things about himself in all the scriptures.

The Liturgy of the Word:
This is the Word of the Lord.
'Discerning the Presence'
PRESENCE: Luke 24:25-27

Listening to the Word of the Lord in the readings of the day, we too are invited to discern the Lord's presence in our lives as he walks with us

- *inviting us to trust*
- *informing us, inspiring us, healing us*
- *making himself present to us*
- *transforming our hearts and minds*
- *affirming our role as God's chosen people.*

As they came near the village to which they were going, he walked ahead as if he were going on. But they urged him strongly, saying, 'Stay with us, because it is almost evening and the day is now nearly over'. So he went in to stay with them.

Affirming our Faith: I Believe. *'Inviting the Stranger'* INVITATION: Luke 24:28-29

Unless we invite Jesus in he will always remain a stranger. He won't force himself into our lives. (ref. The one knocking at the door – which can only be opened from the inside.) Only with an invitation to 'come and stay' can an interesting encounter develop into a transforming relationship – can companions on the journey become companions of the soul. 'I believe . . .' – we are saying a deep, personal 'Yes' not only to the words spoken, but to the One who spoke them. In making this affirmation we are daring to open ourselves to communion.

When he was at the table with them, he took bread, blessed and broke it, and gave it to them. Then their eyes were opened, and they recognised him; and he vanished from their sight. They said to each other, 'Were not our hearts burning within us while he was talking to us on the road, while he was opening the scriptures to us?'

That same hour they got up and returned to Jerusalem;

The Liturgy of the Eucharist: Take and Eat. *'Entering into Communion'* COMMUNION: Luke 24:30-32

Bread taken, blessed, broken, given.

A meal shared, such a common, human gesture, yet a meal transformed into a complete self-giving Communion. God becoming our daily food and drink. God's intense desire to enter into the most intense relationship with us.

'Suddenly the two disciples who ate the bread and recognised him are alone again. But not with the aloneness with which they began their journey. They are alone, together, and know that a new bond has been created between them. They no longer look at the ground with downcast faces. They look at each other and say: 'Did not our hearts burn when he talked to us on the road and explained the scriptures to us?' Communion creates community. Christ, living in them, brought them together in a new way. The Spirit of the Risen Christ, which entered them through the eating of the bread and the drinking of the cup, not only made them recognise Christ himself but also each other as members of a new community of faith. Communion makes us look at each other and speak to each other, not about the latest news, but about him who walked with us. We discover each other as people who belong together because each of us now belongs to him. We are alone because he disappeared from our sight, but we are together because each of us now belongs to him and so has become one body through him . . . Communion creates community, because the God living in us makes us recognise the God in our fellow humans.'

and they found the eleven and their companions gathered together. They were saying, 'The Lord has risen indeed, and he has appeared to Simon!' Then they told what had happened on the road, and how he had been made known to them in the breaking of the bread.

Luke 24:13-35

The Dismissal: Go and Tell.
'Going on a Mission'
MISSION: Luke 24:33-35

Communion leads to missions – that desire to 'go and tell'. Mission first to those 'at home', mission that is expressed in the way we live our eucharistic life. Like those two on the road we have our stories to tell. We have a mission to fulfil and are excited about it, but we have to listen to what others have to say. Then our stories can be told, bringing joy and affirmation, building community, strengthening community for mission.

Based on Henri Nouwen's
With Burning Hearts
Geoffrey Chapman, 1994

The Mass – Our Eucharistic Celebration

Our central act of worship as a community
    with Christ
    in the Spirit
    to the Father

In joy we come, we listen, we give thanks, we take and eat, we go out.

We come in joyful celebration to worship the Lord with his community of believers.

We prepare ourselves for this celebration by acknowledging our sinfulness and asking for forgiveness from God and from the community.
We praise God.
We pray together.

We listen to God's Word.

- First Reading (taken from the Old Testament on a Sunday)
- Psalm
- Second Reading (on a Sunday)
- Gospel Acclamation
- Gospel
  (Year A: Matthew)
  (Year B: Mark)
  (Year C: Luke)
- Homily
- Bidding Prayers

We give thanks

We prepare to offer the gifts of bread and wine, and ourselves, to the Father.

- In the preface we thank God for what he has done for each one of us.
- Full of thanks for God's goodness we praise him in union with the whole Church, saying 'Holy, holy, holy Lord, God of power and might . . .' The priest in the following prayer echoes this song of praise.
- He asks the Father *to send his Holy Spirit* to transform the bread and wine. (The priest puts his hands over the gifts.)
- The *words of consecration* are said. Jesus becomes present in the form of bread and wine.

- Father, we celebrate the *memory* of Christ your Son.
- The *offering* to God of the life-giving bread.
- We ask the *Holy Spirit* to transform men and women into the Body of Christ, to live his life, in a spirit of unity with each other, in and through Christ.
- We pray for people in that Body of Christ – the Pope, the Bishop, the sick, the dead, etc. (Intercessions.)
- We shall sing your glory with everyone, moving towards the Kingdom. 'Through him, with him, in him . . .'

We take and eat

In communion with Christ and with one another we are invited to share, to receive the Bread of Life.

We go forth to make a better world, to share our Christian life and love, nourished and strengthened by Christ's Word and his life-giving bread.

(Source unknown)

For discussion

1. From all that you have heard,
      what surprises you?
      pleases you?
      raises questions?

2. Is there any Sunday Mass that you remember particularly well?
   What made it so special?

3. Is there more we could be doing in this parish to help the children take part more fully in the Mass?

4. Other reflections, comments . . .

> A fully Christian life is unthinkable without sharing in the liturgical action which brings the faithful together to celebrate the paschal mystery. Hence the religious initiation of children should have the same object. The Church, which baptises infants and entrusts them with the gifts conferred by this sacrament, should make sure that they grow in communion with Christ and with the Christian community.
>
> *Directory on Children's Masses* (DO 459)
> Catholic Truth Society, 1973

'I tell you the truth, anyone
who will not receive the
Kingdom of God like a little
child will never enter it.'

Session 3. 'Speak Lord, your servant is listening'

Exploring the Mass – the Liturgy of the Word

General outline

Preparing the session

Focal point

Symbols/pictures reflecting the theme of the session, e.g. table with Bibles and candles, pictures/symbols associated with listening, icon.

Welcome

Welcome the group. Prayer. Invite the parents to introduce themselves to the person sitting on either side. Introduce the team. Explain the plan of the evening (especially time for refreshments!). Invite the parents to share any comments, reflections since the last meeting.

Leading into the theme

Developing the theme ————————> see 'Adults journeying in faith' (page 87)

Reflecting on the theme

Living the theme ————————— see Family Sheet

At home

- Explain what the children are doing with their teacher/catechist and how parents can support this.
- Becoming a 'listening' family: practical suggestions.
- Family prayer.

At Mass

- Focus on the Liturgy of the Word

Looking ahead

- Practicalities concerning   the next children's session
                                      the next parents' meeting.

Celebrating the theme

Explain the next Liturgy – its purpose, what is being asked of the children and their families; practical planning.

Prayer
Using the resources, plan a closing prayer to reflect the theme of the session.

Closing the session
Thank the group for their participation.
Final words . . .

After the meeting
Tidying up and clarifying communication with families not represented at the meeting.

Team preparation
Session 3: Planning sheet

1. Reviewing the last meeting

Questions for reflection   what went well?
                                  with what were you disappointed?
                                  what do you want to do differently?

2. Preparing yourselves

Share together your reflections on 'Pause and reflect . . .'

3. Preparing for Session 3

Date _____ Time _____

Venue _____ Theme _____

Areas of responsibility   **Team member**

Publicity/reminder to parents
of the next meeting   _____

Setting the scene   _____

Focal point   _____

Refreshments   _____

Welcome and introduction   _____

Leading into the theme   _____

Developing the theme   _____

Reflecting on the theme   _____

Living the theme   _____

Closing the session   _____

After the session – tidying up   _____

Contacting absent parents   _____

Resources

Family Sheet: what adaptations?   _____

Worksheets/handouts to be duplicated _____

Page numbers: _____   _____

❏ Flipchart ❏ Felts ❏ Tape recorder _____

 *Session 3: Planning prayer*

Focal point _____

Creating a mood of prayer

lighting a candle	yes/no
taped music	yes/no
taped song	yes/no

Invitation to pray

led by _____

Opening song/prayer

led by _____

Reading   with/without music backing
with/without slides

Pause for reflection   with/without invitation to reread passage
with/without invitation to pick out keywords/phrases

Invitation to share reflection

led by _____

Invitation to share intentions

led by _____

Closing words/song

led by _____

Session 3: Pause and reflect, 1

Set time aside to do this exercise either alone at home or as part of the planning meeting.

I developed this exercise as a result of hearing the story of a priest who went to visit a patient in his home. He noticed an empty chair at the patient's bedside and asked what it was doing there. The patient said, 'I had placed Jesus on that chair and was talking to him before you arrived . . . for years I found it extremely difficult to pray until a friend explained to me that prayer was a matter of talking to Jesus. He told me to place an empty chair nearby, to imagine Jesus sitting on that chair and to speak with him and listen to what he says to me in reply. I've had no difficulty in praying ever since.'

Some days later, so the story goes, the daughter of the patient came to the rectory to inform the priest that her father had died. She said, 'I left him alone for a couple of hours. He seemed so peaceful. When I got back to the room I found him dead. I noticed a strange thing, though; his head was resting not on the bed but on a chair that was beside his bed.'

Try this exercise right now even though at first it might seem childish to you:

> Imagine you see Jesus sitting close to you. In doing this you are putting your imagination at the service of your faith: Jesus isn't here in the way you are imagining him, but he certainly is here and your imagination helps to make you aware of this.
>
> Now speak to Jesus . . . If no one is around, speak out in a soft voice . . .
>
> Listen to what Jesus says to you in reply . . . or what you imagine him to say . . .

If you do not know what exactly to say to Jesus, narrate to him all the events of the past day and give him your comment on each of them. That is the difference between thinking and praying. When we think we generally talk to ourselves. When we pray we talk to God. Do not bother to imagine the details of his face and clothing etc. This might only prove distracting. St Teresa of Avila, who frequently prayed like this, says she could never imagine the face of Jesus . . . She only sensed his nearness as you sense the nearness of someone whom you cannot see in a dark room but whose presence there is clear to you.

This method of praying is one of the quickest means of experiencing the presence of Christ that I know of. Imagine that Jesus is by your side all through the day. Speak with him frequently in the midst of your occupations. Sometimes all you will be able to do is glance at him, communicate with him without words . . . St Teresa, who was a great advocate of this form of prayer, promises that it will not be long before the person who prays in this way will experience intense union with the Lord. People sometimes ask me how they can *meet* the Risen Lord in their lives. I know of no better way to suggest to them than this one.

Sadhana, a Way to God, Anthony de Mello SJ. Gujarat Sahitya Prakash, Anand, 1978

You could adapt this exercise to use with parents

Session 3: Pause and reflect, 2

As this meeting's theme is 'listening to the Word', you might like to prepare yourselves by praying a scripture passage. One is given below. You may prefer to choose Sunday's Gospel.

1. Quietening ourselves, we decide how long to spend in prayer.

2. We place ourselves in God's presence, asking the Spirit to open our eyes, ears, heart and mind to God's Word.

3. We read through the text. (Aloud, if facilities allow for this, so we can listen attentively to the text.)

4. We reread the passage picking out, staying with, meditating on words/phrases that draw us. Hear God speak those words *now*.

   Reading scripture is like receiving a letter from a friend.

   We read it, reread it, reread parts of it, etc.

   Stop where you feel drawn to stop – respond as you feel you want to.

   Don't try to work things out – let God speak through the Word.

5. We let God speak in the silence.

6. We draw our prayer to a close – a gracious leave-taking, just as when leaving a friend – we give thanks – we close with, for example, *Glory be . . .*

7. We share as much as we wish of what we have heard in our hearts with the group; of what has struck *me* today; of how this passage is speaking to me today.

When Jesus received the news of John the Baptist's death he withdrew by boat to a lonely place where they could be by themselves. But the people heard of this and, leaving the towns, went after him on foot. So as he stepped ashore he saw a large crowd; and he took pity on them and healed their sick. When evening came, his disciples came to him and said: 'This is a lonely place and the time has slipped by; so send the people away, and they can go the villages and buy themselves some food.' Jesus replied: 'There is no need for them to go; give them something to eat yourselves.' But they answered, 'All we have with us is five loaves and two fish.' 'Bring them here to me,' he said. He gave orders that the people were to sit down on the grass; then he took the five loaves and the two fish, raised his eyes to heaven and said the blessing. And breaking the loaves he handed them to his disciples who gave them to the crowds. They all ate as much as they wanted, and they collected the scraps remaining. Twelve baskets full. Those who ate numbered about five thousand men, to say nothing of women and children.

Matthew 14:13-21

'Speak Lord, your servant is listening'

Exploring the Mass – The Liturgy of the Word

Preparing to Celebrate Holy Communion

I have a question to ask you, brothers and sisters. Tell me, which do you consider to be of greater value: The Word of God, or the Body of Christ? If you wish to answer correctly, you would have to say that the Word of God is not to be treated as inferior to the Body of Christ. How careful we are that nothing slip from our hand and fall to the floor. But the same care must be taken to ensure that the Word of God, which has been given into our keeping, is never lost to our hearts through our thinking and speaking of other things. The one who is negligent in hearing the Word of God is no less guilty than the one who, through carelessness, allows the Body of Christ to fall to the floor.

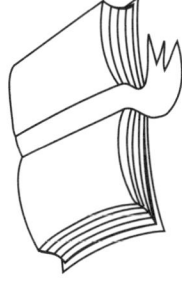

Sermon 78.2

Caesarius of Arles (died circa AD 530)

Family prayer

Take a phrase or sentence of Jesus, and use it for Night Prayers, e.g. 'I want you all to be my friends.' Repeat it a couple of times.

Thank you, Jesus, for always wanting to be my friend.
Thank you for all the other friends you give me, especially . . . .

Help me always to be a good friend of yours.

Prayer

Lord, open my ears to your words
so that I can hear them.
Lord, open my heart to your words
so that I can love them.
Lord, open my eyes
so that I can see you in people.
Lord, give me your strength
to do what your words tell me to do.
Here I am, Lord, speak to me.
Amen.

What is the Liturgy of the Word?

We are invited to open our ears and heart to the Word of the Lord.

First Reading   Usually from the Old Testament. The Word of God spoken to Israel. God's chosen people.

Psalm   We respond trying to make the Word of God our own.

Second Reading   We hear the first Christians tell us what it really means to listen to God's Word in such a way that it becomes a living force in our lives.

Acclamation   We acclaim Christ who is present through the Gospel reading, announcing the Good News.

Gospel   We listen to Christ's words.

Homily   We have the Word spoken in the scriptures broken for us so that it can become part of our lives – we are helped to understand and respond to God's Word.

Creed   This offers us a means of assenting to the Word of God that we have just heard, and want to make our own.

Bidding Prayers   In response to what we have heard we pray for our needs and those of our community.

At home

- Read together the Gospel story. Ask the children, 'What do you think Jesus could be telling us in the story?' Share with them what the message of the story is for you. Sometimes just end a story by saying 'Isn't it wonderful that Jesus loves people enough to do this for them', or for us . . .

- Really become more aware of how you listen to one another at home – whether you really respond and react to what you have heard, or whether it might just as well not have been said from the effect it has.

- When someone comes home from school saying, 'Listen, Mum . . .' or 'Listen, Dad . . . ' try to give an extra couple of minutes just listening, in spite of the meal to be cooked, the washing up to be done, etc. In the long run it will be worth it!

At Mass

- Try to concentrate on the listening parts. Remind the children that we sit down so that we can listen comfortably and quietly.
- Encourage them to join in the response, 'Thanks be to God'.
- Find the response to the Psalm on the Mass sheet and pray it together.
- When it comes to the Gospel Acclamation, remind the children we are going to stand to hear the words of Jesus. He is speaking to each one of us. Find the words of the Alleluia verse so that you can both join in.
- At the end of the Gospel, encourage them to pray with everyone else, saying 'Praise to you, Lord Jesus Christ.'

Dates for the diary

Adults journeying in faith – Catechists' notes

Exploring the Mass – the Liturgy of the Word

Introduce the theme.

> We are invited to listen to God's Word spoken to us in the scriptures. Recall the theme of the last meeting and indicate how this relates to and follows on from it.

A reflection

- Caesarius of Arles (died circa AD 530), 'I have a question to ask you . . . ' (see Family Sheet)

  or

- Recount an incident from your own experience where listening did/didn't take place.

Leading into the theme: describe and explore

Invite the group in twos or threes

- to recall how many times in the last twenty-four hours they have said, 'Why don't you listen?' How do they know when they have/have not been listened to?

  or

- to recall times when they have been changed through listening to someone.

  or

- to name words they would use to describe a good listener.

  or

- Words of scripture (page 89) that mean something special.

Invite the group

- to reflect quietly on the worksheet
- to share any responses they would like to make with their neighbour.

From the feedback, lead into . . .

Developing the theme: listen

A presentation exploring the Liturgy of the Word. The following suggestions may be helpful:

- What is this Liturgy of the Word? (Family Sheet)
- The Church's Year (page 90)
- Different ways God speaks to us today – scripture, prayer, other people, daily life.
- An exploration of the Biblical characters who listened and responded to the Word: Samuel (1 Samuel 3:1-21), Mary (Luke 1:26-38), the disciples, Zacchaeus (Luke 19:1-10), Saul (Acts 9-) . . .

- Jesus – the one who listened to the Father:

Luke 4:1	in the wilderness, before beginning his public ministry.
Luke 4:42	prayer before the calling of the disciples.
Luke 6:12	before the choice of the twelve.
Luke 9:28	the Transfiguration.
Luke 11:1	teaching the disciples to pray.
John 17	the night before he died
Luke 22:39	in the garden.
Luke 23:34	on the cross.

- Jesus – the one who shows us the Father if we listen to him.

Reflecting on the theme: reflect and relate to life
Give each person a copy of the readings for the following Sunday.

Invite the group to

a. read quietly through them all.

b. choose one.

c. spend a little time with it, underline key phrases. Ask yourself, 'What is this saying to me?'

d. imagine they are the Parish Priest . . . if they had to preach on this passage on Sunday, what would they want to say?

Share reflections in small groups.

Feedback. General comments, observations.

(You may want to link this with a discussion on how we can help our children to develop a love of the scriptures or on the reason for sometimes having a separate Liturgy of the Word for children during Sunday Mass.)

These words of scripture are important to some people . . .

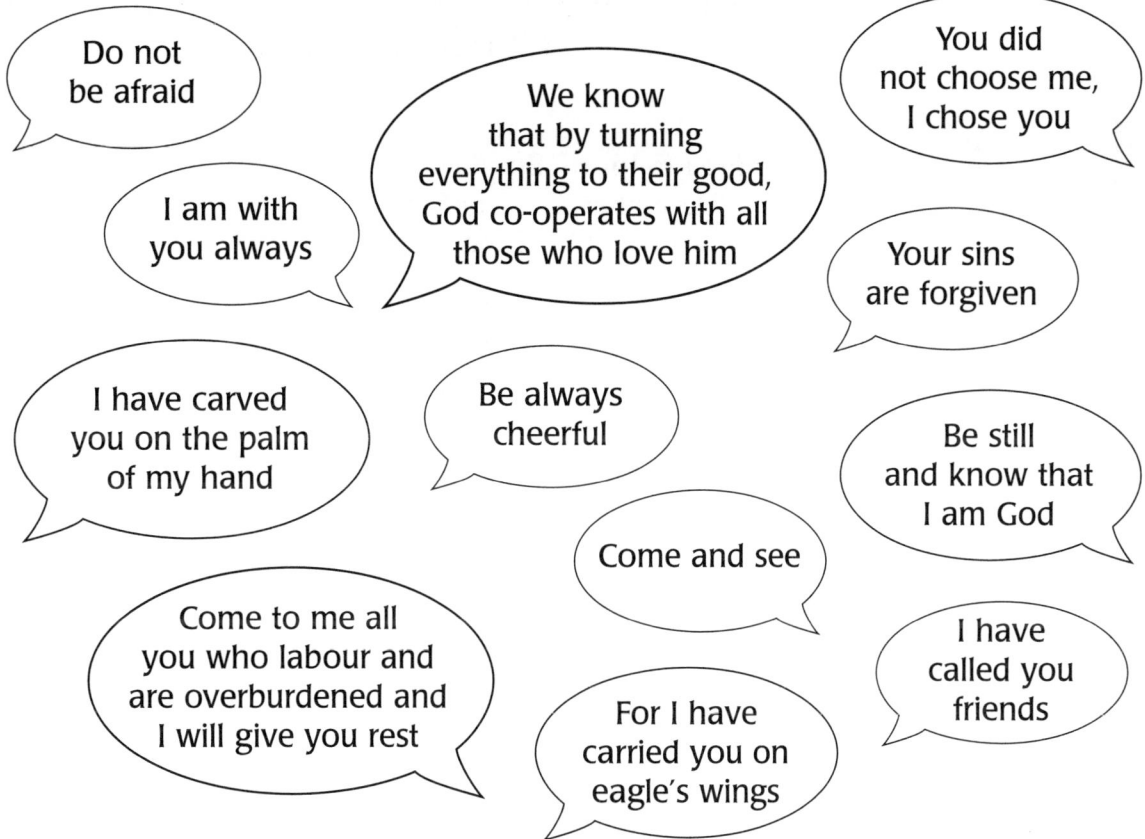

Do not be afraid

I am with you always

We know that by turning everything to their good, God co-operates with all those who love him

You did not choose me, I chose you

Your sins are forgiven

I have carved you on the palm of my hand

Be always cheerful

Be still and know that I am God

Come and see

Come to me all you who labour and are overburdened and I will give you rest

For I have carried you on eagle's wings

I have called you friends

What are some of the words from the scriptures that are important to you?

Why are they important to you?

The Church's Year
(This is reflected in the Liturgy of the Word)

Advent
First to fourth Sunday
8 December – Feast of the
 Immaculate Conception

Christmastide
25 December – Christmas Day
26 December – St Stephen's Day
Sunday after Christmas – The Holy Family
1 January – Mary, Mother of God
Second Sunday after Christmas
6 January – Epiphany
Sunday after Epiphany – Baptism of
 the Lord

Ordinary Time
Sundays

Lent
Ash Wednesday
First to fifth Sunday
Passion (Palm) Sunday
Holy Thursday
Good Friday
Holy Saturday

Eastertide
Easter Sunday
Second to sixth Sunday of Easter
Ascension (40 days after Easter)
Seventh Sunday of Easter
Pentecost Sunday

Ordinary Time
Trinity Sunday
Sundays

Feast Days
Corpus Christi (Thursday after Trinity Sunday)
29 June – Saints Peter and Paul
15 August – The Assumption of Our Lady
1 November – All Saints
2 November – All Souls

Session 4. 'My soul proclaims the greatness of the Lord'

Exploring the Mass – the Liturgy of the Eucharist

General outline

Preparing the session

Focal point

Symbols/pictures reflecting the theme of the session, e.g. two tables – one with a Bible, the other with bread and wine, bulbs/new-life plants, crucifix, symbols of thanksgiving.

Welcome

Welcome the group. Prayer. Invite the parents to introduce themselves to the person sitting on either side. Introduce the team. Explain the plan of the evening (especially time for refreshments!). Invite the parents to share any comments, reflections since the last meeting.

Leading into the theme

Developing the theme — see 'Adults journeying in faith' (page 101)

Reflecting on the theme

Living the theme ———— see Family Sheet

At home

- Explain what the children are doing with their teacher/catechist and how parents can support this.
- Practical suggestions.
- Family Prayer.

At Mass

- Focus on the Eucharistic Prayer.

Looking ahead

- Practicalities concerning the next children's session
  the next parents' meeting.

Celebrating the theme

Explain the next Liturgy – its purpose, what is being asked of the children and their families; practical planning.

Prayer
Using the resources, plan a closing prayer to reflect the theme of the session.

Closing the session
Thank the group for their participation.
Final words . . .

After the meeting
Tidying up and clarifying communication with families not represented at the meeting.

Team preparation
Session 4. Planning sheet

1. Reviewing the last meeting

Questions for reflection   what went well?
with what were you disappointed?
what do you want to do differently?

2. Preparing yourselves

Share together your reflections on 'Pause and reflect . . .'

3. Preparing for Session 4

Date _____ Time _____

Venue _____ Theme _____

Areas of responsibility	Team member
Publicity/reminder to parents of the next meeting	_____
Setting the scene	_____
Focal point	_____
Refreshments	_____
Welcome and introduction	_____
Leading into the theme	_____
Developing the theme	_____
Reflecting on the theme	_____
Living the theme	_____
Closing the session	_____
After the session – tidying up	_____
Contacting absent parents	_____

Resources

Family Sheet: what adaptations? _____

Worksheets/handouts to be duplicated _____

Page numbers: _____ _____

❏ Flipchart ❏ Felts ❏ Tape recorder _____

 *Session 4: Planning prayer*

Focal point _____

Creating a mood of prayer

lighting a candle   yes/no

taped music   yes/no

taped song   yes/no

Invitation to pray

led by _____

Opening song/prayer

led by _____

Reading   with/without music backing
with/without slides

Pause for reflection   with/without invitation to reread passage
with/without invitation to pick out keywords/phrases

Invitation to share reflection

led by _____

Invitation to share intentions

led by _____

Closing words/song

led by _____

Session 4: Pause and reflect

Some reflections shared by Bishop Brian Noble with some catechists, priests and teachers at St Wilfrid's, Northwich on 18 September 1996. After reading this, you might share your responses with the rest of the team.

A REFLECTION ON THE MASS

When invited to address you today, I was left free to select whatever aspect of either of the sacraments I wished to choose. And, as I pondered the topic, my mind went back to my former existence as a parish priest and times with teachers and catechists involved in the First Communion programme. In particular I remembered a new catechist who, at the start of the programme, couldn't understand why there were such themes as 'Belonging', 'Listening', 'Making Peace' and 'Going Forth'. 'What's all that,' she said, 'got to do with Holy Communion?' Clearly it hadn't clicked with her that receiving Communion is part of a bigger picture, and, if truth be known, cannot be correctly understood if separated from the rest of the Mass. Seemingly, it hadn't yet dawned on her that these other themes of belonging and listening and making peace, and so on, were all to do with the other parts of the Mass.

And, remembering that incident reminded me too of where repeatedly the difficulties lay in the Programme, for parents, for children, and indeed for catechists and teachers too. There never seemed to be too much problem with the themes of belonging, listening, making peace, sharing a meal and going forth. The starting point for all of these themes was easy enough. There were clear human experiences which could be used as a launching pad; belonging to families, belonging to the school community; listening to each other, making peace and saying sorry when we've hurt each other and things have gone wrong; sharing a meal in celebration for parties, for Christmas and birthdays, and of course going forth to make a better world, to make others happy. The human experiences for the earthing of these themes was, and is, readily available.

Where the problem lay was in what we might call 'the middle of the Mass' – the Eucharistic Prayer, the Consecration. While there would be a general awareness that all of this had something to do with the Last Supper and something to do with Good Friday and the death of Jesus, it was rarely more focused than that. And not surprisingly therefore, it was difficult to identify any readily available human experience on which to draw for a further exploration of this part of the Mass. And then the danger would be that we would quickly and quietly move away from this, and head into what seemed to be more manageable waters of Communion itself and the family of the Church sharing a meal together.

Well, if none of this in any way resonates with your own experience, so be it! But I suspect that what their experience was, is not uncommon. And, that being so, and feeling moved to rise to a challenge, I though that I would spend a little time trying to take a closer look at this troublesome part of the Eucharist.

Those of you who take an interest in matters theological and were around in the sixties and seventies, might remember that Jesus was often referred to in those decades as 'the man for others'. I think I'm right in saying that the phrase emerged from the writings of Dietrich Bonhoeffer, the Lutheran theologian who died in a concentration camp just before the end of the war. It's a good description of Jesus and one I think all of us would readily recognise as we read through the pages of the Gospels – Jesus, the man for others.

But it seems to me that it does need to be complemented by a description of Jesus as 'the man for his Father'. And that too emerges so clearly from the pages of the Gospel. Indeed I think it must be argued that Jesus was so completely 'the man for others' precisely because he was also 'the man for his Father'. The freedom to be totally for others sprang from his oneness with the Father. Without that sense of the all-importance of God, the sovereignty of God, human beings, we ourselves, inevitably set about promoting ourselves, establishing our own security, defending ourselves, providing for ourselves, and again, almost inevitably, this will be at the expense of others. If I am number one on the agenda then others are bound to be number two. So the contrast between the way of Jesus and the way of those with whom he lived, is very marked, and conflict, especially with the powerful and the influential, was inevitable right from the beginning. The teachings of Jesus, his way of life, what he considered to be all-important, were a direct threat and a challenge to those who held sway in the religious and political establishment. And it shouldn't surprise us that his public life lasted no more than three years. From quite early on it would seem, according to the Gospels, that Jesus began to sense what his fate would be. There was a fundamental incompatibility between his way, his values, his teaching, and the ways of the world.

And bearing in mind all that I've just said, it won't come as any surprise to realise that, far from accepting his death as an unpleasant side effect of his teaching and his way of life, he actually positively went forward to it. Why? Because death would be the final sign of his total confidence in his Father. It would be the final manifestation of his thinking not of himself and his own welfare, but of being totally for others. And so, our second Eucharistic Prayer can say: *'Before he was given up to death, a death he freely accepted. . .'* He went to his death, he died as freely as he had lived. And the night before that death, *'He took bread and gave it to his disciples saying, "This is my Body, given for you"'*. The Last Supper, and what Jesus did on that occasion, can never be separated from, and must never be separated from, all that had gone before and all that was to happen the day after. In giving himself in the Eucharist on that occasion, he was, if you like, giving us his last will and testament, a living reminder, a permanent reminder, of all that he stood for. And so it's no accident that the bread is broken and the blood red wine poured out, for this is none other than the man who was totally for others and totally for his Father – a way of life which costs not less than everything.

And this is the Christ who becomes sacramentally present for us in the Eucharist. Though now risen and glorified, he is still the Christ who lived for the Father and for us. Indeed the way to that fullness of life which he now has as risen Lord, lay precisely through the giving of himself to the Father and to us.

The more we ponder these truths, the more I think we will realise just how central, how all important this particular part of the Mass, and the theme associated with it, actually is in our understanding of the Eucharist. It really takes us to the very heart of what the Eucharist is all about. And if we aren't deeply aware of it, there is a very real danger that our understanding will remain at best superficial, and at worst totally deficient.

And this perhaps we can see most clearly if we move on to look at what might seem to be a straightforward aspect of the Eucharist to understand, namely the Communion itself. Family meal it certainly is but how much more as well. The food we receive is the Jesus we have been describing and our sharing of such Food is itself the sign of the unity which Christ achieved by his life and death. Communion is not so much *my* Communion with Jesus and *your* Communion with Jesus but *our* Communion with each other *in* and through Christ. And that's why we don't just pray quietly on our own at Communion but sing together. We're celebrating together what the Man for Others and the Man for his Father has made us to be – a people at one in him.

Clearly, then, an appreciation of this central part of the Mass, helps us to a richer understanding of Communion. And that is also true for our understanding of the other themes of the Mass. So, for instance, the Liturgy of the Word, especially the Gospel reading, is there to bring home to us, to remind us, of who this Jesus is, of what he stood for. Only after our minds and hearts have been reopened through the Liturgy of the Word, will we be ready and able fully to appreciate the Jesus we are receiving in the Sacrament.

And again, what this receiving him really involves becomes clearer from reflection on his life and his death. To receive Communion is in fact to pledge ourselves afresh to *his* way of life and to *his* values. It is to become like him, a people pledged to be 'for others' and 'for the Father' – to be agents of unity. And again, the cost of such a way of life is clearly spelt out for us in the symbolism of the broken bread and the cup of suffering.

And understanding our Communion in this way does of course bring into sharper focus the importance of the early themes in the Communion Programme, the theme of belonging and the theme of making peace. If we are to be a people 'for others' in the way that Jesus was, then clearly the recognition that we do indeed belong to each other and are part of God's family, is all important. Furthermore, we clearly need to seek reconciliation where relationships have broken down, either our relationships with each other or with God himself.

'Go in peace to love and serve the Lord'. Going forth to make a better world, the dismissal at the end of the Mass, far from being a simple rounding off of the Mass, is an integral part of what the Eucharist is all about. Christ gives himself to us so that we can be strengthened, formed into his own image and likeness more thoroughly and thereby empowered with his Spirit to go out into the world and to live what we have received.

And lest much of what I have said might strike you as being burdensome and over-demanding, we do need to remind ourselves that in the Eucharist it is the risen Christ that we are receiving – the Christ who was born, who lived, who suffered and died, yes, but now the Christ who has been raised to new life in recognition of the validity of his way of life. And now it is empowered by the Spirit of the risen Christ that we are able to live and to carry on his mission. For over twenty-five years now, I've carried around with me a quotation from the writings of Hans Kung which sums up much of what we've been exploring: *'In the light and power of Jesus we are able, in the world of today, to live, to act, to suffer and to die in a truly human way because we are totally dependent on God and totally committed to our fellow human beings.'*

All very well, you may say, but that still leaves us with the rather difficult task of translating some of this into manageable terms for the parents and children with whom we're dealing at the time of First Communion. Yes, I recognise the problem and have indeed experienced it but perhaps the first and greatest hurdle of all is to allow these truths to sink deep into ourselves.

Rt Rev Brian Noble
Bishop of Shrewsbury
18 September 1996

'My soul proclaims the greatness of the Lord'

Exploring the Mass – The Liturgy of the Eucharist

Preparing to Celebrate Holy Communion

The 'Last Supper' Story

St Matthew tells us about a very special meal Jesus shared with his friends the night before he died.

The disciples did as Jesus told them. They prepared the paschal celebration.

When evening came, Jesus sat at the table with the Twelve. As they were eating he said, 'Truly, I tell you, one of you will betray me . . .' Later during the meal Jesus, having taken the bread and blessed it, broke it and gave it to his disciples saying, 'Take this and eat it! This is my body.'

And having taken the cup and given thanks, he gave it to them, saying, 'Drink this, all of you! For this is my blood. The blood of the Covenant that is given for many for the forgiveness of their sins. I tell you, I will drink no more of this fruit of the vine until the day when I will drink the new wine with you in the Kingdom of God.'

Matthew 26:19-21, 26-29.

Experience Jesus Today, Albert Hari and Charles Singer Novalis
Matthew James Publishing, JPH, 1993

Each time we gather together to celebrate Mass we remember this meal. Jesus is with us.

Family prayer

Before you begin this prayer make yourself still.
Ask God to help you to pray.

Listen to Mary's words:
'My soul proclaims the greatness of God.'

Think of all the things for which you want to thank God.

Prayer

For all that our parents give to us,
we give you thanks, O Lord, our God.
For the love and the care
that many people show to us,
we give you thanks, O Lord, our God.
For the smiling faces
and the friendship of those who love us,
we give you thanks, O Lord, our God.
For those who bring us close to you,
we give you thanks, O Lord, our God.
Amen.

Christ is really present to us in the bread and wine. Under the signs of bread and wine he is sharing with us himself, his love and his life, totally and completely.

He offers himself to us, to be taken by each one of us so that he may be intimately present in each of our hearts and lives – those of the whole of the community of believers.

Christ is not present 'just to be there'. He is present to give himself to us and to be accepted by us so that he may truly live in us and we in him.

For Reflection

- When you hear the phrase 'new life' what does it mean to you?

- Can you think of a Gospel character whose life was transformed or renewed through meeting Christ?

- Who are the people who have transformed your life, brought you new life?

- Can you remember a time when you came away from Mass feeling uplifted or renewed?

At home

- To help deepen a sense of gratitude in the children, look for opportunities for giving thanks and praise.
- People who love one another give of themselves for and to others through daily actions. We can help the children to deepen their understanding of this through helping them to become more aware of how people at home, friends, etc., 'give' to one another.

At Mass

- Encourage the children to join in the responses, particularly at the beginning of the *Eucharistic Prayer*, the *Holy, Holy, Holy*, the *Great Amen* and the *Acclamation* at the Consecration.
- Point out how at the Consecration we bow our heads in thanksgiving and adoration for Christ's presence with us in this way.

Dates for the diary

Adults journeying in faith – Catechists' notes

Exploring the Mass – the Liturgy of the Eucharist

Introduce the theme – relate/link it to the two previous sessions, Exploring the Mass. Recall the purpose of the two tables – the focal point of tonight's meeting is the second one – the theme of thanksgiving.

A reflection:

> *For I received from the Lord what I also handed on to you, that the Lord Jesus on the night when he was betrayed took a loaf of bread, and when he had given thanks, he broke it and said, 'This is my body that is for you. Do this in remembrance of me.' In the same way he took the cup also, after supper, saying, 'This cup is the new covenant in my blood. Do this, as often as you drink it, in remembrance of me.' For as often as you eat this bread and drink the cup, you proclaim the Lord's death until he comes.*

1 Corinthians 11:23-26

Leading into the theme: describe and explore

- Can you list ten things that happened in the last week for which you said, 'Thank God' (page 102)? 'Buzz' with neighbour and compare notes.

  or

- Eucharistic Prayer II (pages 103-104) – Give out copies. Explain that this is one of the ten in regular use at the moment. (Eucharistic Prayers I, II, III, and IV, two for Reconciliation, three for Children and one for Special Occasions.)

Invite the group to underline all the words referring to 'praise', 'thanks' and 'new life'. Then compare notes with their neighbour. Invite general comment/feedback leading to . . .

Developing the theme: listen

A presentation exploring the Liturgy of the Eucharist. The following resources may be helpful:

- 'Eucharist' means thanksgiving. For what are we coming together to thank God? (*Your Faith,* Redemptorist Publications, 1993, pp. 64-65).
- Jesus gives thanks to the Father: Matthew 11:25; Mark 8:6; Luke 22:17-19; John 6:11.
- Real Presence (page 105).
- Real Presence and Holy Communion (page 106).
- *God for Grown-ups*, Redemptorist Publications, 1995, Section 29.

Reflecting on the theme: reflect and relate to life

Invite the group to reflect in small groups on all they have heard, using the questions on the Family Sheet.

Drawing together.

Can you list ten things that have happened this week that caused you to say 'Thank God'?

Thank God . . .

Let everything that has breath, PRAISE the LORD!

Eucharistic Prayer II

Introduction

The Eucharistic Prayers are the result of a long history. We are told that at the Last Supper Jesus 'gave thanks' to his Father. That, in essence, is what these prayers are all about. But as the Church grew and spread from that intimate group, so the way of 'giving thanks' developed into stylised structure. We can best appreciate it if we look at Eucharistic Prayer II. (All the Eucharistic Prayers have the same structure.)

Preface

In the preface, the Church gives thanks to the Father, through Christ, in the Holy Spirit, for all his works; creation, redemption and sanctification (CCC 1352).

People
Holy, holy, holy Lord, God of power and might,
heaven and earth are full of your glory.
Hosanna in the highest.
Blessed is he who comes in the name of the Lord.
Hosanna in the highest.

The whole community thus joins in the unending praise that the Church in heaven, the angels and all the saints, sing to the thrice-holy God.

(CCC 1352)

Priest
Lord, you are holy indeed,
the fountain of all holiness.
Let your Spirit come upon these gifts
to make them holy,
so that they may become for us
the body and blood of our Lord,
Jesus Christ.

*In the **epiclesis,** the Church asks the Father to send his Holy Spirit (or the power of his blessing) on the bread and wine, so that by his power they may become the body and blood of Jesus Christ and so that those who take part in the Eucharist may be one body and one spirit (some liturgical traditions put the epiclesis after the anamnesis).*

(CCC 1353)

Before he was given up to death,
a death he freely accepted,
he took bread and gave you thanks.
He broke the bread,
gave it to his disciples, and said:
Take this, all of you, and eat it:
this is my body which will be given up for you.

When supper was ended, he took the cup.
Again he gave you thanks and praise,
gave the cup to his disciples, and said:
Take this, all of you, and drink from it:
this is the cup of my blood,
the blood of the new and everlasting covenant.
It will be shed for you and for all
so that sins may be forgiven.
Do this in memory of me.

*In the **institution narrative,** the power of the words and the action of Christ, and the power of the Holy Spirit, make sacramentally present under the species of bread and wine Christ's body and blood, his sacrifice offered on the cross once for all.*

(CCC 1353)

Let us proclaim the mystery of faith.

People
Christ has died,
Christ is risen,
Christ will come again.

Priest
In memory of his death and resurrection, we offer you, Father, this life-giving bread, this saving cup.
We thank you for counting us worthy to stand in your presence and serve you.
May all of us who share in the body and blood of Christ
be brought together in unity
by the Holy Spirit.

*In the **anamnesis** that follows, the Church calls to mind the Passion, Resurrection and glorious return of Christ Jesus; she presents to the Father the offering of his Son which reconciles us with him.*

(CCC 1354)

Lord, remember your Church throughout the world; make us grow in love, together with John Paul, our Pope, N . . . , our bishop, and all the clergy.
Remember our brothers and sisters who have gone to their rest
in the hope of rising again;
bring them and all the departed into the light of your presence.

*In the **intercessions,** the Church indicates that the Eucharist is celebrated in communion with the whole Church in heaven and on earth, the living and the dead, and in communion with the pastors of the Church, the Pope, the diocesan bishop, his presbyterium and his deacons, and all the bishops of the whole world together with their Churches.*

(CC 1354)

Have mercy on us all; make us worthy to share eternal life
with Mary, the virgin Mother of God, with the apostles, and with all the saints who have done your will throughout the ages.
May we praise you in union with them, and give you glory
through your Son, Jesus Christ.

Through him,
with him,
in him,
in the unity of the Holy Spirit,
all glory and honour is yours,
almighty Father,
for ever and ever.
Amen

*In the **final acclamation,** all our prayer is through Jesus to the Father, and so we gather ourselves for the climax of the prayer – the Great AMEN. It means 'I believe', 'I agree'.*

(Rev Peter Morgan)

CCC: *Catechism of the Catholic Church*
pp. 304-305, paragraphs 1352-1354
Geoffrey Chapman, 1994

Real Presence

Let us consider the belief that the Christ is really present in the Eucharist.

It is helpful to remember the Exodus. The Bible tells us about the enslavement of the Israelites in Egypt and their deliverance. We do not need to delve here into the details of the actual historical events. We can remain with the biblical account. There we are told that when the night of their liberation came they were to eat a meal, no doubt in part to be nourished for the journey. They were to eat a lamb without blemish and mark the lintel and doorposts with its blood. That would protect them from the angel of death who was going to destroy the first-born of the Egyptians. They were to eat unleavened bread as well. There was a cup of blessing also. These instructions were fulfilled. The people were delivered. They passed over from their physical slavery in Egypt to the freedom of the promised land. There each year they celebrated their deliverance by eating again that passover meal as a memorial. It was not passive remembering. The memorial took them back to their roots; it affirmed their identity as the people God had chosen as his own.

We come forward many centuries. In an upper room in Jerusalem Jesus is celebrating that passover meal with his disciples. And at the appropriate moments in the meal, when the unleavened bread is broken and distributed and the cup passed round, we are told that Jesus paused and identified himself with these elements: 'This is my body which is for you . . . This cup is the new covenant in my blood . . .' (1 Corinthians 11:24-25). It is impossible to imagine the bewilderment which must have come over the apostles. To them his words must have seemed meaningless.

After the supper they go out. We know what followed. Jesus was arrested, tortured and executed. Then on the third day he rose from the dead and they saw him. Gradually the significance of these events dawned on them. Their ancestors had been saved from slavery in Egypt; they passed over from that slavery to freedom. The risen Christ revealed the salvation of which that earlier deliverance had been only the anticipation. Death had been defeated. And the significance of the supper dawned on them as well. *The meal which had celebrated their ancestors' passover had been transformed.* This new passing over from sin and death to new life in the risen Lord had been expressed in this action: Christ was the Lamb who was slain and whose blood daubed, not the lintel and doorposts, but the wood of the cross, so that all people might be delivered from their slavery to sin and pass over in freedom to the promised land and life of salvation. The unleavened bread and the cup of blessing find their meaning fulfilled by their being identified as his body and blood.

It is essential to remember this background if we are to glimpse what our belief in the Eucharist proclaims. When its origins in the history of the Jews are ignored, it can seem so easily to be arbitrary and unbelievable. The origins in no way explain the mystery of the belief, but they put it in a context which allows us to see more readily what is taking place. The mechanics of a mystery are always elusive. We may nevertheless recognise its truth.

We do not know how Christ is present in the Eucharist; at the same time we believe in the fact of his presence. We believe that he is really present, really present in a sacramental way.

The Catholic Faith, Roderick Strange, Oxford University Press, 1986

Real Presence and Holy Communion

Most of us would not have to think too long if we were asked to explain what we mean by the phrase 'the real presence'. It's part of our Catholic shorthand to describe the specialness of the gift that Jesus has given us of himself, and it flows from our grasp in faith of his words at the Last Supper; 'This is my Body', 'This is my Blood'. He didn't say 'This is like my Body' or 'This will symbolise my Body'. The identity is clear.

Such awareness of faith, for child or adult, doesn't grow merely out of rational argument or reflection – but rather from an experience of the faith that is lived and expressed in a parish at prayer, in sensing the atmosphere of the church as a place of worship, in growing to recognise and love the signs and symbols of our faith that adorn the church, in the example and witness of believers. In our reordered churches we recognise afresh the symbolic meaning of sacred objects: the altar as the focal point and place of sacrifice and meal; the ambo (lectern) from which God's word is spoken to us; the tabernacle, in its proper place, where the sacred hosts are reserved for the sick to be nourished and for the devotion of the assembly. Jesus is really present to his people in each sacred place.

We are present to lots of people in many different ways. We are present to others in memories and thoughts, by letters and phone calls, by Christmas cards and visiting – some presences are more intense than others, but all are in some sense 'real'. That Jesus wanted to be with us, present to us, we know from his own words: 'When two or three are gathered together in my name, I will be there' (Matthew 18:20); 'Whenever you do this to the least of my brothers, you do it to me' (Matthew 25:40; 'I will be with you all days, even to the end of time' (Matthew 28:20); 'I no longer call you servants, but friends' (John 15:15). How special and intimate is his presence among us at Mass when we gather in his name, when he nourishes us with his word, when we gather round the altar and call down his Spirit on the gifts of bread and wine. His presence in the Eucharist is powerful – in gathering us, in teaching us, in praying in us, in nourishing us for our lives. Traditionally we have spoken about his presence in the bread and wine as 'real presence', and that is why we approach these gifts with great respect and veneration. Our communion with the Lord is a moment of great intimacy, and the way in which we pray over and distribute this food and drink expresses our faith that Jesus is present to us in the eucharistic assembly. It is because of our awareness of the specialness of his presence in bread and wine that we treat them with such reverence, but we should be no less reverent to the Word, nor to one another who are temples and tabernacles of the Lord at Holy Communion. Our eucharistic celebration is extended by the reservation of the host in the tabernacle so that the sick and housebound can be linked spiritually with the family of the parish by receiving the gift that Jesus died to give us. The red flame that burns by the tabernacle reminds us of this great gift of sacrificial love, reminds us of the community that we belong to, and invites us to prayers of adoration and praise.

Rev Peter Morgan

106

Session 5. 'Let your light shine'

Exploring the Mass – Going Out from Mass

General outline

Preparing the session

This final meeting can provide an opportunity for thanking, for reviewing, for providing information about parish activities, for inviting people to help with next year's group . . .

Focal point

Symbols/pictures reflecting the theme of the session, e.g. candles and shared table.

Welcome

Welcome the group. Opening prayer. Invite the parents to introduce themselves to the person sitting on either side. Introduce the team. Explain the plan of the evening (especially time for refreshments!). Invite the parents to share any comments, reflections since the last meeting.

Leading into the theme

Developing the theme ⟶ see 'Adults journeying in faith' (page 114)

Reflecting on the theme

Living the theme ———— see Family Sheet

At home

- Explain what the children are doing with their teacher/catechist and how parents can support this.
- Letting the Lord's Light shine! Discuss possible ways of doing this.
- Family Prayer.

At Mass

- Focus on 'Go in peace to love and serve the Lord'.

Looking ahead

- What could happen in the parish in which these families might participate? Discuss this. (Details could be on the Family Sheet.)

Celebrating the theme

Explain the next Liturgy – its purpose, what is being asked of the children and their families; practical planning.

Prayer

Using the resources, plan a closing prayer to reflect the theme of the session.

Closing the session

Thank the group for their participation.

Final words . . .

After the meeting

Tidying up and clarifying communication with families not represented at the meeting. Confirm the date of the team's meeting to evaluate the programme.

Team preparation
Session 5: Planning sheet

1. Reviewing the last meeting

Questions for reflection   what went well?
with what were you disappointed?
what do you want to do differently?

2. Preparing yourselves

Share together your reflections on 'Pause and reflect . . .'

3. Preparing for Session 5

Date _____ Time _____

Venue _____ Theme _____

Areas of responsibility	**Team member**
Publicity/reminder to parents of the next meeting	_____
Setting the scene	_____
Focal point	_____
Refreshments	_____
Welcome and introduction	_____
Leading into the theme	_____
Developing the theme	_____
Reflecting on the theme	_____
Living the theme	_____
Closing the session	_____
After the session – tidying up	_____
Contacting absent parents	_____

Resources

Family Sheet: what adaptations? _____

Worksheets/handouts to be duplicated _____

Page numbers: _____ _____

❏ Flipchart   ❏ Felts   ❏ Tape recorder _____

 *Session 5: Planning prayer*

Focal point _____

Creating a mood of prayer
lighting a candle   yes/no
taped music   yes/no
taped song   yes/no

Invitation to pray

led by _____

Opening song/prayer

led by _____

Reading   with/without music backing
with/without slides

Pause for reflection   with/without invitation to reread passage
with/without invitation to pick out keywords/phrases

Invitation to share reflection

led by _____

Invitation to share intentions

led by _____

Closing words/song

led by _____

Session 5 – Pause and reflect

You might reflect on how celebration for you is liberation.

TO CELEBRATE IS TO LIBERATE

To celebrate is to liberate. We attend Sunday Mass, but we consider it an individual act. We put in our weekly contribution, but we may not open our wallets and hearts to the larger concerns of sisters and brothers of Jesus. We join in the liturgical singing, but we often fail to sing the good in the character of our neighbours afterwards. We thus fail to see that the liturgical celebration looks to the liberation of the community. To celebrate is to liberate.

Deuteronomy insists that to keep the Sabbath is to make the liberating act of the Exodus have an impact in the present. Deuteronomy also singles out the male and female slaves, not as subjects entrusted to the overlord, but as persons to be respected and protected. To celebrate the Sabbath means to honour the dignity of all in the household. Ultimately the overlord must have the same interest in his household as the Lord had for Israel in the Exodus.

Mark presents a Jesus who saw Sabbath observance in terms of human liberation. In the standing grain dispute, Sabbath means the freedom to provide for human needs. In Jesus' view, the institution serves the people, not *vice versa*. In the story of the man with the withered hand, the proper question for Sabbath observance should be: How much good can I do for people? and not: How much good can I refrain from doing? To take part in the Sabbath means to look to the needs of the people. In Mark, Jesus defends the position that to celebrate is to liberate.

Those who respond to the needs expressed in the prayer of the faithful truly celebrate. Those who carry away the gospel message to meet the needs of family and friends really participate. Those who leave church and continue the music by singing the praises of their fellow humans take part in liturgy. Those who hear the scripture readings and leave to promote justice for all are real worshippers. All such people believe that to celebrate is to liberate.

Eucharist celebrates the liberating death of Jesus. Eucharist connects this Jesus with his body, his sisters and brothers. Eucharist insists that the bread and the wine are the symbols of ongoing concern for this body. In Eucharist, too, to celebrate is to liberate.

Homily Notes: Ninth Sunday of Year B
John F. Craghan
Scripture in Church, volume 27, no. 106

'Let your light shine'

Exploring the Mass –
Going Out from Mass

Preparing to Celebrate Holy Communion

'Go, therefore, make disciples of all the nations; baptise them in the name of the Father and of the Son and of the Holy Spirit, and teach them to observe all the commands I gave you. And know that I am with you always; yes, to the end of time' (Matthew 28:19-20).

Family prayer

Before you begin this prayer make yourself still.
Ask God to help you to pray.
Listen to the words of Jesus:
'Let your light shine'.

Think about all the people you know who shine with the light and love of Christ.
Thank Jesus for wanting you to shine with his light,
for wanting you to be his Body here on earth.

Prayer

Christ has no body now on earth but ours,
no hands but ours,
no feet but ours.
Ours are the eyes through which is to shine out
Christ's compassion in the world.
Ours are the feet through which
he is to go about doing good.
Ours are the hands with which
he is to bless all people NOW.

Please help each one of us, Jesus,
to be your body here on earth.
Thank you.
Amen.

St Teresa of Avila (adapted)

'Happenings' in the parish to which you are very welcome . . . .

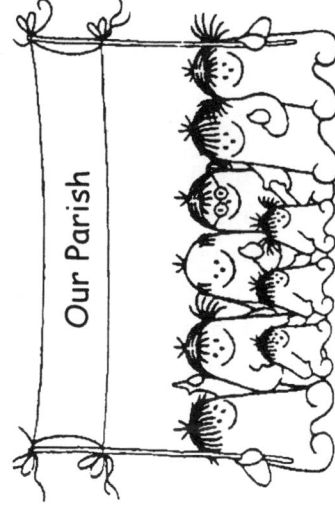

Our Parish

Questions for Discussion

- From all that you have heard, what has

  a. surprised you?

  b. pleased you?

  c. raised questions?

- What have you enjoyed?

- What changes should be made for next year's group?

- In the light of all that you have experienced over the past few months, what observations would you like to share?

Adults journeying in faith – Catechists' notes

Introduce the theme: Exploring the Mass – Going Out from Mass
Go in peace to love and serve the Lord.

A reflection:

Christ has no body now on earth but yours,
no hands but yours,
no feet but yours.
Yours are the eyes through which is to shine out
Christ's compassion in the world.
Yours are the feet through which
he is to go about doing good.
Yours are the hands with which
he is to bless all people now.
(St Teresa of Avila – adapted)

Leading into the theme: describe and explore
The Eucharist doesn't end with receiving Communion.

- Invite the group
  a. to quietly reflect on people whose Christian witness they admire.
  b. to 'buzz' with neighbour, sharing reflections.
- 'What Do You See?' (page 116). What thoughts does this poem provoke?
  Invite the group
  a. to reflect quietly on the poem.
  b. to share any observations they would like to make with their neighbour.

Invite general comments/feedback leading into . . .

Developing the theme: listen
You might find the following resources helpful in preparing your presentation on the theme.

- The call of lay people – their baptismal vocation (page 117).
- Scripture references:
  Matthew 25 The vision
  Matthew 28:16-20 The call
  John 15:12 The command to love
  Luke 11:1-4 The Kingdom comes
  John 13 Service – the washing of feet
  Matthew 18:1-4 Unless you become like little children . . .
  Matthew Various parables – the Kingdom of Heaven is like this . . .
  Micah 6:9 This is what Yahweh asks of you . . .
- The struggles of living as people building the Kingdom, the supports and helps we need, we have . . . (page 118)

Reflecting on the theme: reflect and relate to life
Invite reflection in small groups using the questions on the family sheet.

Feedback. Drawing together.

Refer to the original list of questions raised at the first meeting. Show how these have been responded to.

What do you see?

What do you see, nurse?
What do you see?
Are you thinking when you are looking
    at me,
a crabbit old woman not very wise,
who dribbles her food and makes
    no reply
when you say in a loud voice,
    'I do wish you'd try';
who seems not to notice the things
    that you do
and forever is losing a stocking or
    shoe;
who, unresisting or not, lets you do
    as you will
with bathing and feeding the long
    day to fill.
Is that what you're thinking?
Is that what you see?
Then open your eyes, nurse, you're
    not looking at me.
I'll tell you who I am as I sit here so still,
as I use at your bidding, as I eat at
    your will.
I'm a small child of ten with a father
    and mother,
brothers and sisters who love one
    another.
I'm a young girl of sixteen with wings
    on her feet,
dreaming that soon now a lover she'll
    meet,
remembering vows that I promised
        to keep.
I'm twenty-five now, I have young of
    my own
who need me to build a secure
    happy home.
A woman of thirty, my young ones
    now grown fast,
bound to each other with ties that
    should last.
At forty my young sons now grown
    will be gone
but my man stays beside me to see
    I don't mourn.

At fifty, once more babies play around
    my knee,
again we know children, my loved
    one and me.
Dark days are upon me, my husband
    is dead.
I look to the future, I shudder with
    dread.
My young are all busy rearing young
    of their own.
And I think of the years and the love I
    have known.
I'm an old woman now and nature is
    cruel,
'tis her jest to make age look like a
    fool.
The body it crumbles, graces and
    vigour depart,
but inside this carcass a young girl
    still dwells
and now and again my battered
    heart swells.
I remember the joys, I remember the
    pain
and I'm loving and living all over
    again.
And I think of the years all too few,
    gone too fast
and accept the stark fact that nothing
    will last.
So open your eyes, nurse, open and see
not a crabbit old woman –
look closer, see me.

Anon

On being baptised – some reflections . . .

Because the lay faithful belong to Christ, Lord and King of the Universe, they share in his kingly mission and are called by him to spread that Kingdom in history (CFL 14).

The lay faithful, in fact, 'are called by God so that they, led by the spirit of the Gospel, might contribute to the sanctification of the world, as from within like leaven, by fulfilling their own particular duties. Thus, especially in this way of life, resplendent in faith, hope and charity they manifest Christ to others' (CFL 15).

The eyes of faith behold a wonderful scene: that of a countless number of lay people, both women and men, busy at work in their daily life and activity, oftentimes far from view and quite unacclaimed by the world, unknown to the world's greatest personages but nonetheless looked upon in love by the Father, untiring labourers who work in the Lord's vineyard. Confident and steadfast through the power of God's grace, these are the humble yet great builders of the Kingdom of God in history (CFL 17).

CFL: *Christifideles Laici*, Catholic Truth Society, 1988

And now, what follows for the Church? Today, more than ever, she must live her mission; more energetically than ever she must repulse that narrow and false conception of her spirituality and inward life which would confine her, blind and dumb, to the recesses of the sanctuary.

The Church cannot shut herself up, inactive, in the privacy of her churches and thus neglect the mission entrusted to her by divine providence, the mission to form man in his fullness and so ceaselessly to collaborate in building the solid basis of society. This mission is of her essence.

From this aspect the faithful, more precisely the laity, are in the front line of the Church's life; through them, the Church is the vital principle of human society. Consequently, they particularly must have an ever more clear consciousness, not only of belonging to the Church, but of being the Church.

Pius XII, 1946
in Yves Congar, *Laity, Church and World*
Geoffrey Chapman, 1960

Weak and Wobbly Hearts

Christian action is done by you and me, ordinary people with weak and wobbly hearts who do not have the security of trained skills, etc. I think Christian action and the promotion of the Kingdom is done by those who are afraid of what people will say, who are a bit cowardly, who are a bit diffident about standing up in public, do not have the security of plenty of practice and experience, can be capsized by failure, hurt by remarks, hurt by being ignored; find themselves reacting jealously when they do not want to, are overcome by despair, yet go on loving and trusting. It is the weak and wobbly hearts that Christ chooses, as he chose Peter, James and John – all the disciples. They were not the high-fliers of Galilee or Judea. They were the ordinary folk, capable of love.

Letting Go in Love
John Dalrymple
Darton, Longman & Todd Ltd, 1986

APPENDIX

Resources for prayer
Readings

Various passages from scripture could be used. In addition you might find the following suggestions to be appropriate.

Session 1
One Life
source unknown (see page 123)

How Beautiful is the Mass
Oscar Romero (see page 124)

Session 2
Eucharist
R. Voight/Brennan Manning (see page 125)

Session 3
Bidding Prayers for God's People
Translated by H. Soons and J. Rolo: The Grail (see page 126)

Session 4
The Magnificat (see page 127), or 'Let Me Talk to You after Communion'
in *How to Interest Your Child in the Mass*
M. Quinn, Veritas Family Resources, 1982 (see page 128)

Session 5
'Lord' in *Experience Jesus Today*
Albert Hari and Charles Singer Novalis
Matthew James Publishing, JPH 1993 (see page 130)

Hymns
The numbers refer to *Hymns Old and New with Supplement* (HON) and
Liturgical Hymns Old and New (LITON), both published by Kevin Mayhew Ltd.

Session 1
'Love Is His Word', HON 338, LITON 462

Session 2
'We Come To Share Our Story' (*Song of the Body of Christ*)
David Haas *et al*
Creating God, GIA Publications, 1989

Session 3
'O the Word of My Lord', HON 431, LITON 558

Session 4
'This Is My Body', HON 556, LITON 681

Session 5
'Take, Lord, Receive',
Earthen Vessels, Music from St Louis Jesuits, 1975.
North American Liturgy Resources, Phoenix, Arizona

Closing prayers – see page 131

Blessings – see page 132

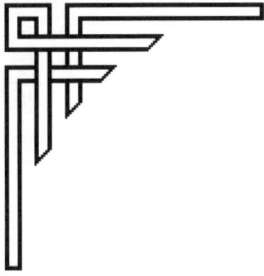

One Life

He was born in a stable, in an obscure village,
from where he travelled less than 200 miles.
He never won an election. He never went to college.
He never owned a home. He never had a lot of money.
He became a nomadic preacher.
Popular opinion turned against him.
He was betrayed by a close friend,
and his other friends ran away.
He was unjustly condemned to death,
crucified on a cross among thieves,
on a hill overlooking the town dump.
And when dead, laid in a borrowed grave.
Nineteen centuries have come and gone,
empires have risen and fallen, mighty armies have marched,
and powerful rulers have reigned.
Yet no one affected men as much as he:
HE IS THE CENTRAL FIGURE OF THE HUMAN RACE,
HE IS THE MESSIAH, THE SON OF GOD, JESUS CHRIST.

Source unknown

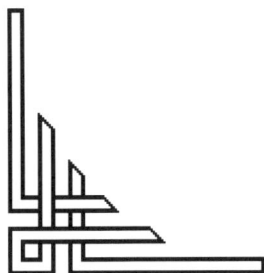

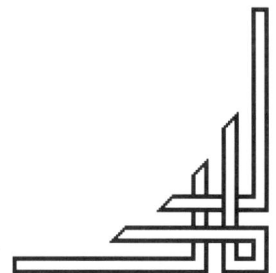

How Beautiful Is the Mass

How beautiful is the Mass,
    especially when celebrated in a cathedral filled
    like ours on Sundays,
or even when celebrated simply
in village chapels with people full of faith,
who know that Christ, the King of Glory, Eternal Priest
is gathering together all that we bring him from
    the week:
sorrows, failures, hopes, plans, joys, sadness, pain!
How many things each one of you,
brothers and sisters, brings to your Sunday Mass!
And the Eternal Priest gathers them in his hands
and by means of the human priest who celebrates,
lifts them up to the Father
as the product of the people's labour.
United to my sacrifice present on this altar
the people are made godlike
and now leave the cathedral
    to keep on working,
    to keep on struggling,
    to keep on suffering,
but ever united with the Eternal Priest,
who remains present in the Eucharist
so that we can meet him the next Sunday also.

The Violence of Love, Oscar Romero
Compiled and translated by James R. Brockman SJ
The Plough Publishing House, 1998

Eucharist

Broaden your understanding of Eucharist beyond the Sacrament

Eleven at night,
  in front of me an old man,
    poking around in a garbage can.
He was hungry.
  I thought 'Eucharist, that's food –
    maybe I'll tell him.'
But the look in his eyes,
  the despair on his face,
    told me to forget it.
So, I smiled, said 'Hi' – and gave him EUCHARIST.
She was cute,
  nice build, a little too much paint,
    wobbly on her feet as she slid from her barstool, and on the make.
'No, thanks, not tonight,' – and I gave her EUCHARIST.
She lived alone,
  her husband dead, her family gone.
And she talked at you, not to you,
  words, endless words, spewed out.
So I listened – and gave her EUCHARIST.
Downtown is nice,
  lights change from red to green, and back again.
Flashing blues, pinks and oranges. I gulped them in,
  said, 'Thank you, Father,' – and made them EUCHARIST.
I laughed at myself, and told myself,
  'You, with all your sin, and all your selfishness,
  I forgive you, I accept you, I love you.'
It's nice, and so necessary to give yourself EUCHARIST.
And if you can't, if you hurt too bad,
  go to your spouse, go to your friend, go to your rectory,
  and receive their EUCHARIST.
My Father, when will we learn – you cannot talk EUCHARIST –
  you cannot philosophise about it. YOU DO IT. YOU DO IT.
You don't dogmatise EUCHARIST.
Sometimes you laugh it, sometimes you cry it, often you sing it.
Sometimes it's wild peace, then crying hurt, often humiliating,
  never deserved.
You see EUCHARIST in another's eyes, give it in another's hand held tight,
  squeeze it in an embrace.
You pause EUCHARIST in the middle of a busy day,
  speak it in another's ear.
Listen to it from a person who wants to talk.
For EUCHARIST is as simple as being on time
  and as profound as sympathy.
I give you my supper,
  I give you my sustenance, I give you my life,
    I give you me, I give you EUCHARIST.
Give EUCHARIST to others and an unbelieving world will find faith.
We are loved by God and that love overflows to our neighbour.
We are EUCHARISTED by Jesus Christ
  and that EUCHARIST overflows to our neighbour.

R. Voight and Brennan Manning

Bidding prayers for God's people

In these bidding prayers we want to name people
    and through their names bring them before God.
We think of people among us like Adam who gave
    names to all he saw and all he experienced.
We think of people among us like David.
    He took time to sing before God.
We think of strong women among us who are like Judith.
    She took great risks in the struggle against injustice.
We pray for people among us like Job
    who did not know what to do with the heap of rubble in his life.
We pray for people among us like Moses,
    he maintained God's law in the midst of decay.
Among us are people like the prophet Elijah.
    He was fed up with life and began a new life.
Older people among us are perhaps like Enoch
    who went walking every day with God
    and went so far that one day he was seen no more.
There are great believers among us like Abraham
    who listened so well that he could understand you.
We recall as well disbelievers like Jonah
    who barred the way until he found his way.
We may also recall people among us like Mary.
    She allowed things to happen to her
    according to your Word.
We commend to you those who are like Jacob
    broken in the hard wrestle with you.
And caring people among us like Joseph
    who forsaw the needs of all.
We commend them all to you.
Finally we commend to you all
    who try to have the characteristics of Jesus,
    that they become human and serve unto death.
God, all these people are yours;
    the brave, the hesitant, the anxious,
    the joyful, the glad, the believers, the disbelievers too.
Everyone is searching in his or her own way
    for unity and freedom with you.
May we all find you in eternity.

The Grail
Translated by H. Soons and J. Rolo

126

The Magnificat (Luke 1:46-55)

My soul glorifies the Lord,
my spirit rejoices in God, my Saviour.
He looks on his servant in her lowliness;
henceforth all ages will call me blessed.

The Almighty works marvels for me.
Holy is his name!
His mercy is from age to age,
on those who fear him.

He puts forth his arm in strength
and scatters the proud-hearted.
He casts the mighty from their thrones
and raises the lowly.

He fills the starving with good things,
sends the rich away empty.

He protects Israel, his servant,
remembering his mercy,
the mercy promised to our fathers,
to Abraham and his sons for ever.

from *The Divine Office*

'Let me talk to you after Communion . . .'

The text could be
1. illustrated with slides
2. spoken against a background of quiet music
3. different voices could read different sections.

Invite the group to place/imagine themselves into the scene:

> '. . . it's Sunday evening. All the family are busy doing their own thing. Peace reigns at last . . . ! You are just about to turn on the television when something makes you stop and sit quietly. Your mind goes back to Mass this morning . . .'

Slide
1. I tried to catch your attention this morning. Remember when you came back to your seat and closed your eyes and put your head reverently down and talked and talked and talked to me?

2. I wanted to tell you to open your eyes and look at my broken body all around you.

3. I tried to catch your attention that time your toddler stood on the seat and spoke to you, but you gave me a dirty look and humiliated me and didn't hear me.

4. I was the unmarried mother at the end of your seat,

5. the old man in front of you,

6. the family of seven children across the aisle from you and I almost had the impression you disapproved of me.

7. I was the woman in the green coat whose husband left her this week and whose heart was being eaten out right through Mass, and a friendly word would have been a little support to me.

8. I am your wife who cooked and prepared and coped with the children and all the burdens of the house while you read the Sunday newspaper and then went out.

9. I am your husband and children and you stumped and huffed and gave us your cold silent treatment for three-and-a-half long hours after Mass, which blackened and deadened the whole atmosphere of our home.

10. I am your father and mother, and you have ignored and mocked and criticised and tortured us as only a teenager knows how.

11. I am your teenage son in whom you've lost belief and your nagging is driving me crazy.

12. I am your next-door neighbour whom you spend so much time gossiping about and criticising.

13. I am your fellow-parishioner whom you meet every day in the street and you ignore me, busy about your own concerns.

14. And it sickens me, all the coldness, all the squabbling and division and those endless running battles that scourge me and crown me with thorns.

15. And then you pierce my side at Holy Communion with your empty words of love. If you love me, feed my sheep, my starving sheep! And start in your own home.

16. Please don't keep me at bay any longer. Don't talk to me. LISTEN. I don't want you to go on loving my spirit and ignoring my body.

17. I don't want you to open your mouth to receive my body and close your eyes and ears to shut it out.

18. When will you understand that you cannot have Communion with me if you don't have communion with your brothers and sisters in your own family and in your parish?

19. Stop thinking of me as some kind of spiritual being in the skies.

20. I am one with these people and you cannot have me without them.
&
21. On the last day, I won't ask you how many times you attended Mass; that is not your holiness. I will ask you how your family and neighbours fared, how your spouse and children grew in love and faith. How did they live their Mass?

22. How did your family spread its love across your neighbourhood?

23. *Please.* Open your eyes and ears and make the time *to be my Church, to be my body here on earth.*

How to Interest Your Child in the Mass, M. Quinn
Veritas Family Resources, 1982

LORD

Greater than leprosy
that wears out body and heart,
greater than scorn
that judges without pity,
greater than sin
that takes control of us,
your love is wider
than the sky and the earth,
Jesus, Christ, Lord!

Greater than selfishness
that makes us want to keep
everything for ourselves,
greater than hate
that nails the living to a cross,
greater than death
that makes the living fearful,
your life is stronger
than the night and the tomb,
Jesus, Christ, Lord!

Your friends are gathered here
with joy to help those who long
for justice, to share with the needy,
to spread mercy,
to lift up those who are afflicted,
to establish truth, to build a world
of peace and tenderness!

Here we are, Jesus, Christ, Lord,
to proclaim your Word in our cities
and homes and to all the children
of the world!

Experience Jesus Today
Albert Hari and Charles Singer Novalis
Matthew James/JPH, 1993

Closing Prayers

1.
Our Father

2.
Lord God,
you give us Eucharist,
food for our journey
as we respond to your call
to act justly,
to love tenderly
and to walk humbly with you.
For this great gift
we thank you. Amen.

3.
O Lord our God,
you have sown in us your word,
given us your Son –
he, who was broken and died for us,
is bread and life
for the world.
We ask you
to let us find strength to tread his path,
so let us be for each other
as fertile as seed
and as nourishing as bread and thus
    lead a happy life.
Your Word is Near
Huub Oosterhuis
Paulist Press, 1968

4.
For the bread
that gives everlasting life,
nourishment so we can love
God with all our strength
and our neighbour as ourselves.
For offering us your body,
thank you, our Lord!

For the wine
that gives everlasting joy
and strength to spread happiness
among all our brothers and sisters.
For offering us your blood,
thank you, our Lord!
For the Eucharist
that proclaims your glory.
For you, Christ Jesus,
who came to invite all the children
of the world to your celebration.
For you, Christ Jesus
who are always with us,
thank you!
Experience Jesus Today
Albert Hari and Charles Singer Novalis
Matthew James/JPH, 1993

5.
Christ has no body now on earth but
    yours,
no hands but yours,
no feet but yours.
Yours are the eyes through which is to
    shine out
Christ's compassion in the world.
Yours are the feet through which
to go about doing good.
Yours are the hands with which
he is to bless all people now.
St Teresa of Avila – adapted

Blessings

1.
The hands of the Father uphold you.
The hands of the Saviour enfold you.
The hands of the Spirit surround you.
And the blessing of God Almighty,
Father, Son and Holy Spirit,
uphold you evermore. Amen.

> *The Edge of Glory*
> David Adam
> Triangle/SPCK, 1985

2.
May God bless us and keep us.
May God let his face shine on us and be
  gracious to us.
May God uncover his face to us and
  bring us his peace.

> Numbers 6:24-26
> (adapted)

3.
May the blessing of almighty God,
the Father, the Son and the Holy Spirit
be with us as we return home
to love and serve the Lord. Amen.

4.
May the light of your soul guide you.
May the light of your soul bless the
    work you do with the secret
    love and warmth of your heart.
May you see in what you do the beauty
    of your own soul.
May the sacredness of your work
    bring healing, light and renewal
    to those who work with you and
    to those who see and receive
    your work.
May your work never weary you.
May it release within you wellsprings
    of refreshment, inspiration and
    excitement.
May you be present in what you do.
May you never become lost in the
    bland absences.
May the day never burden.
May dawn find you awake and alert,
    approaching your new day
    with dreams, possibilities
    and promises.
May evening find you gracious and
    fulfilled.
May you go into the night blessed,
    sheltered and protected.
May your soul calm, console and
    renew you.

> *Anam Cara*
> John O'Donohue
> Bantam Press, 1997

Recommended reading

One Bread, One Body
Catholic Bishops' Conferences of
England and Wales, Ireland and Scotland
Co-published by the Catholic Truth
Society, London, and Veritas
Publications, 1998

A Parish Pastoral Directory, chapter 8
Ed. William Dalton
The Columba Press, 1995

Sacraments Revisited, chapter 5
Liam Kelly
Darton, Longman & Todd, 1998

Can You Drink This Cup?
Henri Nouwen
Ave Maria Press Inc., 1996

With Burning Hearts
Henri Nouwen
Darton, Longman & Todd, 1994

Focus on the Sacraments
Peter Wilkinson
Kevin Mayhew Ltd, 1987

Catechism of the Catholic Church
Part 2, section 2, chapter 1, article 3
Geoffrey Chapman, 1994

How to Survive Being Married to a Catholic
Redemptorist Publication, 1986

In Celebration of Love
Poster meditation series
St Paul Multimedia Productions, 1997

The Mass
Redemptorist Publication

Your Child's First Communion
Redemptorist Publication, 1990

Your Faith
Redemptorist Publication, 1993

So Much to Celebrate
Tony Castle
Kevin Mayhew Ltd, 2000

Celebrating with Children
Sister Joan Brown
Kevin Mayhew Ltd, 1999

Acknowledgements

The publishers wish to express their gratitude to the following for permission to include copyright material in this publication:

Bantam Press, a division of Transworld Publishers, 61-63 Uxbridge Road, London, W5 5SA, for the extract from *Anam Cara* by John O'Donohue, 1997.

The Catholic Truth Society, 40-46 Harleyford Road, Vauxhall, London, SE11 5AY, for the extracts from *Christifideles Laici; The Pope Teaches – The Pope in Britain,* and *Directory on Children's Masses.*

Geoffrey Chapman, an imprint of the Continuum International Publishing Group Ltd, Wellington House, 125 Strand, London, WC2R 0BB, for the extracts from *Catechism of the Catholic Church; With Burning Hearts,* Geoffrey Chapman 1994, and *Laity, Church and World,* by Yves Congar, 1960.

The Columba Press, 93 The Rise, Mount Merrion, Blackrock, Co. Dublin, Eire, for the extract from *A Parish Pastoral Directory,* ed. William Dalton, Columba Press, 1995.

Darton, Longman & Todd, 1 Spencer Court, 140-142 Wandsworth High Street, London, SW18 4JJ, for the extracts from *Letting Go in Love* by John Dalrymple, published and © 1986 Darton, Longman & Todd Ltd. Bible quotations taken from the *Jerusalem Bible,* published and © 1966, 1967 and 1968 by Darton, Longman & Todd Ltd, and Doubleday & Co. Inc.

Dominican Publications, 42 Parnell Square, Dublin 1, for the John F. Graghan 'Homily Notes'; 9th Sunday of Year B, taken from *Scripture in Church,* vol. 27, no. 106, Dominican Publications.

The Grail, c/o Lesley Toll, 23 Carlisle Road, London, NW6 6TL, for the extract from *The Grail* and *The Magnificat,* © The Grail (England).

Gujarat Sahitya Prakash, Anand, Gujarat, 388 001, India, for the extract from *Sadhana, a Way to God* by Anthony de Mello SJ, 1978.

HarperCollins Publishers, 77-85 Fulham Palace Road, London, N1 1RD, for the diagram (Family Sheet, Session 2), adapted from *Together We Communicate,* Collins 1982.

International Commission on English in the Liturgy, 1522 K Street, N. W. Suite 1000, Washington D.C., 20005-1202, USA, for excerpts from the English translation of *The Roman Missal,* © 1973, International Committee on English in the Liturgy, Inc. (ICEL); excerpts from the English translation of Rite of Penance, © 1974, ICEL; excerpts from the English translation of *Eucharistic Prayers for Masses of Reconciliation,* © 1975, ICEL. All rights reserved.

Matthew James Publishing, 19 Wellington Close, Chelmsford, Essex, CM1 2EE, for the extracts from *Experience Jesus Today* by Albert Hari and Charles Singer Novalis, 1993, and various illustrations.

Rev Peter Morgan.

The National Committee for Gibran, New York, for the extract from *The Prophet* by Kahlil Gibran, published by William Heinemann Ltd, 1926.

Rt Rev Brian Noble.

Oxford University Press, Great Clarendon Street, Oxford, OX2 6DP, for the extract from *The Catholic Faith* by Roderick Strange, Oxford University Press, 1986.

Paulist Press, 997 MacArthur Blvd, Mahwah, NJ 07430, for the extract from *Your Word is Near* by Huub Oosterhuis, 1968.

The Plough Publishing House, Robertsbridge, East Sussex, TN32 5DR, for the extract from *The Violence of Love* by Oscar Romero, 1998.

RCL Enterprises Inc., 200 Bethany Drive, Allen, Texas 75002, USA, for the extract from *The Hour of the Unexpected* by John Shea, © 1977 RCL Enterprises Inc.

SCM Press, 9-17 St Albans Place, London, N1 0NX, for the extract from *Christianity Rediscovered* by Vincent Donovan, SCM Press, 1978.

SPCK Publishing, Holy Trinity Church, Marylebone Road, London, NW1 4DU, for the extract from *The Edge of Glory* by David Adam, SPCK 1985.

St Joseph's Pastoral Centre, St Joseph's Grove, The Burroughs, Hendon, London, NW4 4TY, for the extract by Rosemary McCloskey and June Edwards, © Rosemary McCloskey & June Edwards, St Joseph's Pastoral Centre, Diocese of Westminster.

Veritas Publications, 7-8 Lower Abbey Street, Dublin 1, Ireland, for the extract from *How to Interest Your Child in the Mass* by M. Quinn, first published and © by Veritas Family Resources. Used by permission.

Every effort has been made to trace the owners of copyright material and we hope that no copyright has been infringed. Pardon is sought and apology made if the contrary be the case, and a correction will be made in any reprint of this book.